Judaism Without Christianity

An Introduction to the System
of the Mishnah

Judaism Without Christianity

An Introduction to the System
of the Mishnah

JACOB NEUSNER

KTAV Publishing House, Inc.
Hoboken, NJ
1991

Library of Congress Cataloging-in-Publication Data

Neusner, Jacob, 1932-
    Judaism without Christianity : an introduction to the system of
the Mishnah / Jacob Neusner.
       p.   cm.
    "An abridgement of Judaism, the evidence of the Mishnah."
    Includes bibliographical references.
    ISBN 0-88125-333-2
    1. Mishnah—Criticism, interpretations, etc.   I. Neusner, Jacob,
1932-   Judaism, the evidence of the Mishnah.   II. Title.
BM497.8.N475   1989
296.1'2306—dc20   89-24649
                                        CIP

Manufactured in the United States of America

This book is an abridgement of

Judaism: The Evidence of the Mishnah.

First edition: Chicago, 1981: University of Chicago Press.
Paperback edition: 1984. Second printing, 1985. Third printing, 1986.

Second edition, augmented: Atlanta, 1987:
Scholars Press for Brown Judaic Studies.

Hebrew:

Hayyahadut le'edut hammishnah.

Tel Aviv, 1987: Sifriat Poalim.

Italian translation: Turin 1992 Editrice Marietti.

For
Rabbi Max Roth
Sarasota
in friendship

CONTENTS

Part Two
THE SECOND CENTURY
Social Vision

PREFACE

Judaism as we have known it for nearly two thousand years treats the Mishnah as the first document of the Torah preserved in memory, of the Oral Torah, revealed by God to Moses at Sinai. Put forth in ca. A.D. 200, the Mishnah, seen by itself, presents a complete and encompassing system, a Judaism consisting of a way of life, a world view, and a doctrine of the Israel to whom the system is addressed. In this book I describe, analyze, and interpret that system in its own terms. My claim is that Judaism set forth in the Mishnah constitutes a Judaism formed in response to a particular set of problems. The Judaism of the Mishnah—that is, that system represented by the authorship of the Mishnah—focuses upon the critical and urgent question of whether and how, despite the loss of the Temple of Jerusalem in 70 and the defeat of the effort to regain the city and rebuild the temple in 132–135, Israel retained that sanctity that the Temple had embodied. The answer to that question, self-evidently valid to the Israel that received the Mishnah and made it the foundation of its corporate life, was simple. Israel remains holy, as before, and in diverse, important aspects of its life expresses the sanctity with which, to begin with, God had endowed the holy people.

Since the framers of ideas and laws now found in the Mishnah, working from somewhat before the destruction in 70 to approximately a century afterward, chose as their critical issue the question of Israel's holiness, we ask ourselves what alternative issues faced them. The obvious answer, from our perspective, directs attention to the challenge of Christianity, with its doctrine of another Israel, beside the Israel after the flesh, of a realized salvation in the person of Jesus Christ, risen from the dead, and its holy writings, over and above the Hebrew Scriptures known, in due course, as the Old Testament. In time to come, Christianity would indeed present to the Israel addressed by Mishnah a critical and urgent question: who are you, now that we

xi

are here? But in the time of the Mishnah, the first two centuries of the Common Era, Christianity represented to the sages of the Mishnah no pressing problem. That fact rests on one piece of evidence: the Mishnah itself.

For, as we shall see, that document addresses its questions in its way, and not the Christians' questions in their terms. Later on, by contrast, sages' heirs in the Talmud of the Land of Israel, ca. A.D. 400, Genesis Rabbah, ca. A.D. 400, and Leviticus Rabbah, ca. A.D. 450, as well as other important writings, would indeed take up point by point precisely the issues addressed to the Jewish people by the Christian Church. They would develop a doctrine of the Messiah and of Israel's salvation, which the Mishnah does not offer. They would work out a myth of the revelation of the Torah at Sinai in two media, oral and written, which the Mishnah does not know. They would spell out the identity of the Israel whom God had singled out, which the Mishnah does not trouble to specify. In providing doctrines of salvation, revelation, and Israel (equivalent to ecclesiology), sages represented by the Talmud of the Land of Israel, Genesis Rabbah, Leviticus Rabbah, and related writings of the late fourth and fifth centuries answered questions asked by the age of Christianity's triumph. The shape and structure of their Judaic system contrasts with the Mishnah's Judaism. For that Judaism speaks of not salvation but sanctification, not history and the end of time but nature and the supernatural. Its issues are those framed not by Christianity, with its remarkable restatement of Israel's tradition of prophecy and apocalypse, but by a different crisis altogether. The Mishnah shows us what Judaism might have looked like, had Christianity not attained the astonishing success in the Roman empire represented by the conversion of the state and government to the worship of Jesus Christ. That accounts for the title of this book, which alleges that, in the system of the Mishnah, we discern the shape and structure of a Judaism formed utterly out of relationship with the issues turned from chronic to acute by the triumph of Christianity.

This book is a precis and an abbreviation of my *Judaism: The Evidence of the Mishnah.* It is meant to make the book accessible to a broader audience than the scholarly one for which it originally was written. By omitting most technicalities, I mean to address people with no knowledge at all about Judaism. All that is needed is an interest in how, in the first two centuries of the Common Era, one of the great religions of the West took shape and produced its principal document beyond Scripture (the "Old Testament"). For, as you will learn in this book, just as in these same centuries Christianity came into being and created its first and definitive expressions, so did Judaism as we now know it. It is the story of the beginnings of Judaism as we now know it, that I tell.

Why anyone might want to know how Judaism in its present form began is not self-evident. After all, I speak of times long past. As you will see soon enough, the tragic events of the age have long since been surpassed, in the scale of human disaster many times over, particularly in our own day. Even though one might make the case that what then happened has shaped the life of the Jewish part of the human race to now, mere curiosity is not apt to sustain your interest to the end. What should retain your attention is shared experience, both at the center of the ancient world about which I write, and the world in which today we live. I refer to the experience of passage from high hope to bitter disappointment. I speak of a world at the end of an old and long-established order and the beginning of an age lacking all precedent, all points of reference and orientation. This book is about losers, people who lost the world they and their ancestors had known. But the losers also were survivors. If you want to know how humanity responds to life lacking compass, all center and sense, and yet survives, how people live in a world that has lost its moorings and endure, read this book. For when old landmarks crumbled and were swept away, second century Israel made new maps and set out new markers, through an act of surpassing will.

With the human issues of the age clearly before us, we are apt to be drawn on into matters of detail particular to the time of which we speak. We shall find detail if not interesting, at least important, when we recall that even when their life is expressed only in little and curious things, the life we too share is expressed. My conviction is that the human experience captured by some very odd and remote documents addresses issues both immediate and illuminating. That is why I thought it important to present in this book parts of the other one, suitably revised where necessary, pertinent to the main point. To begin with, in the Foreword, let me describe in broad outline the principal traits of the two centuries at hand, and then explain the argument of this book.

FOREWORD

First-century Jews in the Land of Israel looked for a messiah, expected any day. They undertook great and terrible wars in their quest. Defeated once for all by the end of the first third of the second century in 135, the Jews found little reason to hope for a messiah any more. In the aftermath of crushing defeat, it is difficult to know what anyone was willing to do. The first century was a time of high hope and courageous deed. The second century was an age of disillusion and despair. In the first century people fought wars. In the second some made plans and dreamed dreams. In the first century Israel did things and produced disaster. In the second Israel's sages wrote a book. They produced the document formative and definitive of the religion and thought of Judaism, Israel's world-view and way of life, from then to now.

The first century for the Jewish nation was a time of concrete action in the real material world of sword and blood. The second century was an age of system-building, making things up in the mind, spinning a web of reality out of the gossamer threads of attenuated hope. It was a time of philosophy, inner reconstruction. The first century called forth politicans, generals, holy men and heroes—doers all. The second demanded those who could conceive life beyond despair, imagine utopia and make laws about constructing it here and now—dreamers all. The first century drew to its close—effectively, at the end of Bar Kokhba's war—with the Jewish people glutting the slave markets, the southern part of their Land in ruins, villages and farms up for grabs. The world had not been saved by a messiah but ruined by whatever messiahs Israel had followed. The second century came to an end— effectively, with the formation of a book, the Mishnah, some time around A.D. 200—with the Jews in the Land enjoying limited self-government under a Roman client of their own people, living at peace in their farming villages, contending with the leadership of learned men who brought renewal and inaugurated a protracted age of reconstruction. Generals destroyed. Men of learning (there was scarcely a woman among the sages, and none by the end of the second century) built. Messiahs projected a history and promised to conclude it. Sages spoke of what was permanent and on-going, made the end of history depend upon doing what exactly they said—hence, in the nature of things, postponing it, really, forever.

Only severe, irreversible defeats succeeded in driving from the proscenium of Israelite consciousness people who made promises and tried to keep them. The end of the old order alone won the nation's attention for people who insisted on much and promised little. The first century looked for change and made history. The second century dreamed of permanence and avoided it. Its legacy is a set of laws, governing and describing how things should be. Its message to us is a tale of order. It promises an account of predictable and reliable things. It speaks of a world at rest. It describes the pattern of a society aiming at perfection and sanctification, just as, when things were very good at the beginning, God had sanctified it all. When all things had come to rest, there would be no history at all. The gift of the first century is the example of courage and martyrdom on the battlefield. The enduring endowment of the second century is the lesson of building a holy people and the law for living the holy life called Judaism.

We can speak of the events of the first century down to 135, but only the ideas of the second to 200. We may describe the history made in the first century, but only the vision of eternity—lawful, unchanging life, posited by the philosophers of the second.

Rapidly and in general terms, let us begin by reviewing the principal events in Judaism in the two centuries. These are only three: (1) the first war against Rome, from 66 to 73, with its climax in August, 70, in the destruction of the Temple of Jerusalem, the abrogation of its sacrificial order, the burning of the city, and the capture and slaughter, or enslavement of masses of people; (2) the second war against Rome, from 132 to 135, with its still greater human disaster and its aftermath of brief repression and the permanent closing off of Jerusalem from Jewish access; and (3) the formation of the Mishnah and its adoption as the constitution and law-code of Jewish government of the Land of Israel toward the year 200. These are the three events—two wars and a book—that set the boundaries around the period in which Judaism took shape, in the forms in which we have known Judaism, from that time to this.

In the first century, as I said, a great many Jews in the Land of Israel looked for and expected a messiah. Whether he would be a wonder-worker and teacher of righteousness, a general, a God-man, hope for his coming provoked people to action. Some left their homes and families and followed a messiah. Others joined together in military or monastic bands. For all it was a time for vigorous action, in the belief that history approached its climax and its end. So there were things to be done.

In the earlier part of the second century, these same hopes for God's intervention in the life of Israel in its Land came to a crescendo in the war led by Ben Kosibah, whom some called Bar Kokhba, son of a star. The aftermath of the calamity of that last messianic war for the Jews of the Holy Land in ancient times proved to be a defeat of more than this-worldly proportions. For the Jews of the Land lost not only a war. Gone for good was the Temple and the on-going life of celebration, service to God, animal-offerings and other, concretely to link to God enthroned on high. Since the Temple flourished, with brief interruption, for more than eleven hundred years, we cannot but stand in awe at the change that then had proved to be final.

To understand the gravity of the change, we recall that for eleven centuries and more, the Jewish people had organized its entire life— social, metaphysical, natural and supernatural—around the Temple. The cult had marked off the passage of time and the seasons through the punctuation of slaughtering sacrifices of sheep and cows. Israel had recognized the hierarchy of its society by reference to priests and Levites. Three times a year all Israelites were supposed to come to Jerusalem, and many did at least once in a year. These climactic moments, marking the passage of the natural year and the celebrating of the formative moments in Israel's national life with God as well, infused the Israelites' life with meaning, made sense of nation and nature all at once. Nor should we forget that, in ancient times, meat generally was eaten in a cultic setting, as part of a meal served to God and shared with God. Consequently, these massive gatherings in Jerusalem, with their exalted moments of celebration and their out-pourings of petition, their thanks for what God had given and their beseeching for what God now must give, the processions and parades, with their bonfires and their barbecues—these defined the order of life. In the Temple, in Jerusalem, Israel celebrated God and creation, humanity and the nation, and also ate heartily and well. What was left of the calendar that had marked off the passage of seasons as sacred, had linked the spatial arrangements of the world—where one might walk, for how far—with the cosmic order of the moon and the passage of time, was mere memory. With its system of celebration and cult permanently in ruins, all that Israel had was the memory of the celebration and the hope for the restoration of the cult.

These then are the two centuries and the great event that form the center of interest in this book, the first century, with high hopes and capacity for vigorous undertakings, the second century, with no hope left. Israel lost the first war against Rome, the one fought from 66 to 73 and marked, in 70, by the Romans' destruction of Jerusalem and its Temple. But in the aftermath of that war Israel was not a defeated people. As we see, Israel lost more than a war when the Romans took Betar in 135. Israel as a whole never fought another war in ancient times, though some Jews did from time to time. So in the second century Israel became a defeated people. To study Judaism—the way of life and world view of people who claimed to be Israel—in the period at hand is to discover what happens to people who lose big.

The story of Israel in these two hundred years speaks of foreign things. But it addresses a human situation entirely within the imagination, and even experience, of a fair part of humanity, I mean, the world's losers. Whether the loss is a war and a nation, as with the American South, conquered provinces for so long afterward and not even allowed to reflect upon what might have been; or the loss of a certain frame of mind, a psychology of dominance of the world of ideas and the spirit, as with the invisible empire of the New England mind in religion and literature, the issue is perennial and painful. At hand is a shared experience, far deeper and more enduring in the shaping of consciousness and culture, I think, than the passing moment of triumph.

For to win is fleeting. To list the great empires, past and present, is to repeat the banal exercise of speaking about the transience of glory, the impermanence of success: Assyria, Persia, Greece, Rome, Mongolia, Tartaria, Portugal, Spain, France, Britain, America, Russia, Israel of David and of the Maccabees. Empires measure time in decades, a few, perhaps, for a century. But history's losers, if they persist to remember at all, resentfully reflect for age upon age on what they were and what now they are. Disappointment and despair are the norms of the human consciousness and condition for those nations that persist to remember. The others have it worse. They do not survive to remember, whether Assyrians, Incas, Aztecs, or Norsemen.

We now come to what makes the story of Judaism in the first two centuries important, not merely pertinent. Israel in the centuries under study in this book found a way to deal with defeat. Here I propose to tell what that way is, how it came into being, why it is worth the attention of people who come to the end of a century of unspeakable defeat and take up the burdens of the age beyond. Ancient Israel, in the first and second centuries, discovered how to confront and overcome the end of everything that mattered, how to deal with ultimate chaos and total and complete confusion and disorganization. In the aftermath of two World Wars and many smaller ones, imagining for good reason the end of civilization as we know it, we had better listen to the teaching of that ancient, tough people. If, less than a generation beyond the murder of one third of all of the Jews in the world in Europe in World War II, it may be said, as it is said, "For a Jew, it is a sin to despair," then the Jewish people has learned something worth sharing. If, finally, out of the total nihilism of mass extermination the Jewish people could find the will to build and sustain even a state and nation of its own, then the Jews have something to teach the other defeated people of the world, the rest of the victims and survivors that constitute humanity.

The critical point came in the second century, as I said, with the final and conclusive catastrophe: the Temple site ploughed over, Jerusalem barred to Jews, the entire way of celebrating creation and living by revelation and aiming at redemption a mass of broken blocks and sealed-off ruins. For within one generation, the foundations had been laid for Judaism as we know it, that is, that religion that Jews have kept and that has kept them for the rest of their history, to the present day. It was a way for losers and survivors, remarkably appropriate to their condition then, unhappily congruent to the condition of humanity then and now. We had best listen to anyone who can teach us how to hope and not despair.

This brings us to the first fruit of the fantasy of order in an age of chaos, the book which, on the other side of the abyss of war and defeat, points toward Judaism as we know it. The principal interest in this account of the formation of Judaism in the first two centuries centers upon the Mishnah. That fact speaks out of the title of the book of which the present work is a precis and abbreviation. So let me introduce the Mishnah.

Before we know what the Mishnah is, we want to know why it is important to know what it is. The answer to that question leaps out of the simple equation that follows:

$$\frac{\text{Old Testament}}{\text{New Testament}} = \frac{\text{Written Torah (Hebrew Scriptures)}}{\text{Oral Torah (Mishnah and its continuators)}}$$

The equation would speak more eloquently if you knew what is meant by the elements of the right side of the equation. The top line on both sides speaks of the same holy book, but with the words particular to Christianity and Judaism, respectfully. That is to say, the biblical books that Christians know as "the Old Testament," Judaism knows as the Written Torah. Clearly, in both religious traditions, the reason is that there is another holy book, complementing and completing the Hebrew Scriptures. In the former case, as everyone knows, it is the New Testament. In the latter, as only a few people realize, it is the Oral Torah. The principal myth of Judaism is that when Moses ascended to Mount Sinai, God revealed to him two Torahs, which,

together, constitute "the one whole Torah" of Moses. One of the two
was in writing. The other was formulated and transmitted not in
writing, but through oral transmission and memorization. The Mishnah
is the first and principal expression of this other Torah, the oral Torah
revealed to Moses at Sinai. All of the books of Judaism produced
beyond the Mishnah, in particular, the Talmuds of the Land of Israel
and of Babylonia, rest upon the Mishnah and so constitute parts of
that Oral Torah. So far I have explained why it is important to know
what the Mishnah is. The reason is that the Mishnah constitutes the
first document of the form of Judaism that has predominated from the
time of the Mishnah to our own day, replacing all that had gone before,
absorbing all that would come afterward, into a single mythic structure
and legal-religious system.

But when we know *why* it is important to know what the Mishnah
is, we still know nothing at all about the Mishnah. For, as soon as the
document comes into view, the things said about it become less
interesting (let alone credible) than the things it says, that is, the world-
view which it expresses. The bulk of this book is an effort to describe
that world view, explaining how it took shape, its principal stimuli,
sources, and emphases, and what it meant to the people who made it
up. So it would not serve to attempt in a few words to say what will
take a great many anyhow. What you have to know at this point is a
few very simple facts.

First, the Mishnah is a law code, in the sense that it contains
statements about things we should do and not do.

Second, the Mishnah is a book of religion, in the sense that it speaks
in large part about religious things, holy days, deeds, duties.

Third, the Mishnah is systematic and orderly, presenting a complete
and cogent statement.

Whether or not the world of its day conformed to its system, the
system itself is what matters. That is where we find our way into the
imagination and sensibility of the framers of the document. What
counts in their consciousness and conscience. In the end what we want
to know is how those men solved the problem of their day, because, as
I said, it has turned out to be a perennial and painful problem long
afterward, and not only for Israel. How to recover order when everything seems disorderly, how to build when the ground beneath is
trembling, how to look forward when there is little reason to—this, in
mind, is what they reckoned to do.

Judaism in its first two centuries came into being on the other side
of two wars, and produced, as its first and enduring testimony, a book
of law and religion, a book to express a system of philosophy and a
theory of society. Since the Mishnah emerges in a time of wars, the
one thing we should anticipate is a message about the meaning of

history, an account of events and their meaning. Central to the Mishnah's system should be a picture of the course of Israel's destiny, in the tradition of the biblical histories—Samuel, Kings, Chronicles, for instance—and in the tradition of the prophets of ancient Israel, the several Isaiahs, Jeremiah, and the rest. The Mishnah's principal insistence is the opposite. It speaks of what is permanent and enduring: the flow of time through the seasons, marked by festivals and Sabbaths; the procedures of the cult through the regular and enduring sacrifices; the conduct of the civil society through norms of fairness to prevent unjust change; the pursuit of agricultural work in accord with the rules of holiness; the enduring invisible phobias of cultic uncleanness and cleanness. In the Mishnah there is no division devoted to the interpretation of history. There is no pretense at telling what had just happened. There is scarcely a line to address the issue of the meaning of the disasters of the day.

The Mishnah does not address one-time events of history. Its laws express recurrent patterns, eternal patterns as enduring as the movement of the moon and sun around the earth (as they would have understood it) and as regular as the lapping of the waves on the beach. These are laws on ploughing, planting, harvesting; birth, marriage, procreation, death; home, family, household; work, rest; sunrise, sunset—not the stuff of history. The laws speak of the here and now, not of tradition, past or future. Since, in the time in which the ideas of the Mishnah took shape, most other Jews expressed a keen interest in history, the contrast cannot be missed. The Mishnah imagines a world of regularity and order in the aftermath of the end of ancient certainties and patterns. It designs laws after the old rules all were broken or had fallen into desuetude. It speaks of an eternal present—generally using the continuous present tense and describing how things are—to people beyond all touch with their own past, its life and institutions. Its message, then, is clear.

Part One

THE FIRST CENTURY
Sectarian Origins

1

THE FIRST CENTURY:
THE END OF TIME

The Issues of the Age

The concrete historical facts which shaped the history of every particular kind of Judaism of the first century are few but beyond dispute. They are, first, that the Temple was destroyed in 70 in the midst of a major war against Rome; second, that three generations later, a second war against Rome produced the definitive exclusion of Israelites from Jerusalem and priests from the ruins of the Temple; leading, third, to the final recognition that, for some time to come, after over a thousand years there would be no Temple and no cult. To the best of my ability, behind the internal evidence of the Mishnah itself, I adduce, in evidence of any concern I impute to the framers of the Mishnah, or assign to their program, or invoke in explanation of things they wished to say, only these three facts. All my other statements about the history of Judaism of the particular kind under discussion emerge only from an entirely inductive reading of the literary evidence itself.

Clearly, I do not claim to describe the state of mind and mode of life of the entire Jewish group ("people"), let alone of all those who, in the later first and second centuries, wished to call themselves "Israel." The reason is merely that we lack adequate evidence; it is not that such an encompassing account would not be interesting. It would be not only interesting but also decisive in making sense, also, of the particular corpus of evidence here under close examination. For in the end what the Mishnah redactors imagined must stand up against the reality, recorded independent of their fantasies, the objective political, social, and material reality in which they formed their dreams and designed their account of "Israel" and its life. This we cannot do, much as we want to.

3

Indeed, if we have to posit a large-scale social movement attested to in the evidence we do have, that is, the deeds of masses of people, we must take for granted it is not a movement shaped by the Mishnah but the movement of messianic hope represented by the successive generations of fighters for Israel's freedom from Rome. For two mass actions, about the program and concrete deeds of which we are exceedingly well informed in the main (if not in all desired detail), are the great movements culminating in wars against Rome. Now we have no evidence produced by the fighters themselves about what people were thinking who in 66–73 and again in 132–35 left their homes and fought, risking all and losing all. Incising on their coins, "The Freedom of Israel Year 1," they tell us something altogether too general. Further, our surmise, based on our own rough calculation that three generations—nearly seventy years—were allowed to pass from war to war, that the principal motive for the Second War had to do with the realization of the hopes for repeating the extraordinary pattern narrated in the biblical story of the first Temple's destruction and the people's suffering, atonement and restoration, also is too general. For we do not have first-hand documents which tell us what the participants in the mass movements of Israelite Palestine had in mind in doing what they did. So we cannot describe the world view and the way of life—that is, the "Judaism"—of the generality of Jews who really did shape the history of their nation and their part of the country in the period under study.

It nonetheless seems to me self-evident that their state of mind more nearly will have been expressed by the visionaries whose writings are assembled under the names of Baruch and Ezra (not to mention the vast literature of the apocalypse and historiosophy of the period before 70) than it can be before us in the pericopes of the Mishnah. The reason is simple but compelling. Nothing in the Mishnah and its description of the Israelite world and way of life makes provision for, or leads us to expect, what the people really were doing in the first half of the period in which Mishnah took shape. Jews fought two massive wars against Roman armies in the Holy Land. So the Jewish people in the age of prologue to the Mishnah were making history. Nothing in the Mishnah explains why people should have made wars. So the framers of the Mishnah were avoiding it. The Mishnah is not a plan for that construction of the world which will make ample place for the kind of history that the Jews then wanted to make and did make. Its critical issues are elsewhere than on the battlefield.

The Mishnah's framers' deepest yearning is not for historical change but for ahistorical stasis. Their notion of a holy deed does not encompass the battlefield as the normal setting for consecration. The principal lines of structure, the main beams of order, of the Mishnaic system follow the outlines of the village and the cult, two places in which, in the nature of things, world-shaking historical events of politics and war are alien. For both are locations for an ongoing life, in which events are the uneventful; in the village, birth, marriage, childbearing, death; in the cult, the regular routine, precise and orderly everyday offering of the produce of the field and the village. What is dangerous in the village is the moment at which, for instance, a woman leaves one status and enters some other. What is threatening in the village is change in the status of one person because of the violence or avarice of another. All things have their place; all produce has its price, no more, no less, than true value. In such a world where is there place for "the Freedom of Israel Year 1"? And what can such a concept of freedom have meant to people whose principal document was the Mishnah, where the word *freedom* does not appear even one time (excluding a single play on words)? So the Mishnah is a document whose system cannot have impressed the mass of Israelites in the time in which the system was taking shape. There was then another norma- tive—norm-setting—Judaism than "Mishnaic Judaism."

First-Century Apocalypse

The only extant documents originating in the decades immediately after the destruction of the Temple in A.D. 70 are 2 Baruch and 4 Ezra. We make better sense out of what people did do when we know what they did not do, but what others among their contemporaries did, in response to the same crisis. That is why we must dwell on the writings of other Jews of the Land of Israel, besides those represented in the Mishnah. For if we ask how the character of the Mishnah's system for "Judaism" differs from that of the writings of other Jewish thinkers of the same general period, the first and second centuries after the destruction of the Temple, we have only 2 Baruch and 4 Ezra for comparison. Those writings give some perspective on the work of the framers of the Mishnah, even though they have absolutely nothing in common with the Mishnah. Still, it is in precisely the same period and under essentially common conditions that the authors of Baruch and Ezra choose one set of topics, which they treat in a particular way, and the earliest framers of the Mishnah choose another set of topics, to be treated in a quite different way. If we wish to know what the Mishnah does not discuss, all we need to do is to list the issues and concerns we have seen in writings in the names of Baruch and Ezra— and vice versa.

The crisis precipitated by the destruction of the Second Temple affected both the nation and the individual, since, in the nature of things, what happened in the metropolis of the country inevitably touched affairs of home and family. What made that continuity natural was the long-established Israelite conviction that the fate of the individual and the destiny of the Jewish nation depended upon the moral character both of the one and of the other. Disaster came about because of the people's sin, so went the message of biblical history and prophecy. The sins of individuals and of nation alike ran against the revealed will of God, the Torah. So reflection upon the meaning of the recent catastrophe inexorably followed paths laid out long ago, trod from one generation to the next. But there were two factors which at just this time made reflection on the question of sin and history, atonement and salvation, particularly urgent.

First, with the deep conviction of having sinned and the profound sense of guilt affecting community and individual alike, the established mode of expiation and guilt and of atonement for sin proved not inadequate but simply unavailable. The sacrificial system, which the priestly Torah describes as the means by which the sinner attains forgiveness for sin, lay in ruins. So when sacrifice turned out to be acutely needed for the restoration of psychological stability in the community at large, sacrifice no longer was possible—a crisis indeed.

Second, in the awful August of A.D. 70, minds naturally turned to August of 586 B.C. From the biblical histories and prophecies emerged the vivid expectation that, through the suffering of the day, sin would be atoned, expiation attained. So, people supposed, just as before, in three generations whatever guilt had weighed down the current generation and led to the catastrophe would be worked out through the sacrifice consisting of the anguish of a troubled time. It must follow that somewhere down the road lay renewal. The ruined Temple would yet be rebuilt, the lapsed cult restored, the silent Levites' song sung once more.

Now these several interrelated themes—suffering, sin, atonement, salvation—from of old had been paramount in the frame of the Israelite consciousness. A famous, widely known ancient literature of apocalyptic prophecy for a long time had explored them. The convictions that events carry preponderant weight, that Israelites could control what happened through their keeping, or not keeping, the Torah, that in the course of time matters will come to a resolution—these commonplaces were given concrete mythic reality in the apocalyptic literature. Over many centuries in that vast sweep of apocalyptic-prophetic writings all of the changes had been rung for every possible variation on the theme of redemption in history. So it is hardly surprising that, in the aftermath of the burning of the Temple and cessation of the cult, people reflected in established modes of thought upon familiar themes. They had no choice, given the history of the country's consciousness and its Scriptural frame of reference, but to think of the beginning, middle, and coming end of time as it was known.

Before examining ways in which the question of the age came to be phrased in apocalyptic writings, let us rapidly review the following statement, by Morton Smith, of the world view represented in the common faith of Israelite culture and religion in the Land of Israel, in all its forms and expressions, down to the destruction of the Temple and for some time thereafter. This passage is important to our understanding of the setting in which the several types of Judaism came to expression, because it tells us the convictions common to them all, the world envisaged by each. It places into context, in particular, those reflections on the meaning of the destruction of the Temple which the apocalyptic prophets and poets left behind as testimony to the prevailing frame of mind of the common folk of the country, I mean, the people who fought the two major wars against Rome. So this is what the world was like for that large part of Israel responsive to the vision and poetry of apocalypse:

> The picture of the world common to Jesus and his Jewish Palestinian contemporaries is known to us from many surviving Jewish and Christian documents. It was wholly mythological. Above the earth were heavens inhabited by demons, angels, and gods of various sorts (the "many gods" whose existence Paul conceded in I Cor. 8:15, and among whom he counted "the god of this age," II Cor. 4:4). In the highest heaven was enthroned the supreme god, Yahweh, "God" *par excellence,* who long ago created the whole structure and was about to remodel, or destroy and replace it. Beneath the earth was an underworld, to which most of the dead descended. There, too, were demons. Through underworld, earth, and heavens was a constant coming and going of supernatural beings who interfered in many ways with human affairs. Sickness, especially insanity, plagues, famines, earthquakes, wars, and disasters of all sorts were commonly thought to be the work of demons. With these demons, as with evil men, particularly foreign oppressors, the peasants of Palestine lived in perpetual hostility and sporadic conflict, but the relations were complex. As the Roman government had its Jewish agents, some of whom, notably the Herods, were local rulers, so the demons had their human agents who could do miracles so as to deceive many. The lower gods were the rulers of this age, and men who knew how to call on them could get their help for all sorts of purposes. So could women, whose favors they had rewarded by teaching them magic and other arts of civilized life. On the other hand, Yahweh, like the demons, was often the cause of disasters, sickness, etc., sent as punishments. He sometimes used angels, sometimes demons, as agents of his anger, and his human agents, his prophets, could also harm as well as help. Most Jews believed

that in the end he would destroy or remodel the present world, and create a new order in which the Jews, or at least those who had followed his law, would have a better life. However, as to the course of events and the actors in the coming catastrophe, there was wide disagreement; any number of contradictory programs circulated, with various roles for one or more "messiahs"—special representatives of Yahweh—anti-messiahs, and assorted mythological monsters.

This was the picture of the world *common* in first century Palestine. Even Herod Antipas, the Romans' puppet prince in Galilee, is said to have thought Jesus was John the Baptist raised from the dead. Even Josephus, a Jew of the priestly aristocracy who as a young man was sent on a mission to Rome, held beliefs of this sort; he was proud of the Jews' control of demons; he claimed to have prophetic powers himself and to have prophesied that the Roman general, Vespasian, would become emperor and rule all mankind; and he saw Vespasian as a messiah foretold by at least some biblical prophecies. His own prophecy was famous; the Roman historians Suetonius and Dio Cassius reported it. Suetonius and Tacitus say that such messianic prophecies were common throughout the Near East. We should presume that almost all Palestinian Jews of Jesus' time thought themselves involved in the mythological cosmic drama. [Smith, *Jesus*, pp. 4–5]

Smith's general account of the frame of mind of the Jews of the Land of Israel provides ample justification for turning to the two Pseudepigraphic expressions of this "apocalyptic Judaism" which posited as mythic cosmic drama and which flourished both before and after 70. In a way entirely consistent with a general and prevailing drama, the visionaries before us tell us how, in particular, that ancient and pervasive mode of thought responded to the events of 70.

Thus do 4 Ezra and 2 Baruch introduce us to the mentality of the kind of Judaism predominant both before and in the encounter with the destruction of the Temple. The former Pseudepigraph records visions shown to Ezra in Babylonia (ca. 450 B.C.). The principal theme is how a righteous God causes Israel to fall by the hand of a pagan nation. Sin is the reason, and the theme produces reflection of a psychological character on the nature of human impulse to do evil. The writer sees a conflict between giving the Torah and the character of the people to whom it is given, since, it is clear, that people are unable to carry out the Torah. The destruction proves the impossibility of doing right. The tension is resolved in the belief that at the end of the present age, which is near, a new age—as Smith pointed out—will dawn in which the righteous will be able to keep the Torah. The seven visions of the book go over this same ground of history and its coming conclusion. The same familiar question is asked by 2 Baruch, phrased eloquently, about Israel's suffering and Israel's enemies' prospering. The answer is that the world to come is for the righteous. The recent destruction is a mark that the age is hastening to an end.

Because these two documents are cited merely for illustration and are not critical to the account, which is to come, of the evidence of the Mishnah on the formation of Judaism, I shall treat them very cursorily, first quoting current scholarship for a picture of what the apocalyptic prophets have to say about the events of 70, then simply citing passages in general illustrative of these prophets' overall frame of mind. A complete account of Judaism in the period under discussion would have to do much more here than what is needed for the modest picture of one kind of Judaism, yielded by the evidence under discussion in this book.

Charlesworth provides the following summary of 2 Baruch:

> Most scholars have divided the book into seven sections, with some disagreement regarding borderline verses: an account of the destruction of Jerusalem (1–12); the impending judgment (13–20); the time of retribution and the subsequent messianic era (21–34); Baruch's lament and an allegory of the vine and the cedar (35–46); terrors of the last time, nature of the resurrected body, and the features of Paradise and Sheol (47–52); Baruch's vision of a cloud (53–76); Baruch's letters to the nine and a half tribes and to the two and a half tribes (77–87). The pseudepigraphon is important for numerous theological concepts, e.g. the explanation that Jerusalem was destroyed not by enemies but by angels (7:1–8:5); the preoccupation with the origin of sin (15:5f., 23:4f., 48:42, 54:15, 19; 3 Ezra 7:116–131); pessimism for the present (85:10); the contention that the end will not come until the number of those to be born is fulfilled (23:4–7; cf. 4 Ezra 4:35–37); the description of the resurrected body (49:1–51:6); and the varied messianic concepts. [Charlesworth, *Research*, p. 84]

The following sizable excerpt from the vision attributed to Baruch, Jeremiah's disciple at the time of the first destruction, and generally attributed to a writer who lived in the decades after 70, will serve to portray the frame of mind of survivors. It expresses the perplexity of the age as if affects the destiny of the people of Israel:

> Blessed is he who was not born,
> Or he, who having been born, has died.
> But as for us who live, woe unto us,
> Because we see the afflictions of Zion,
> And what has befallen Jerusalem.

I will call the Sirens from the sea,
And ye Lilin, come ye from the desert,
And ye Shedim and dragons from the forests:

Awake and gird up your loins unto mourning,
And take up with me the dirges,
And make lamentation with me.

Ye husbandmen, sow not again;
And, O earth, wherefore givest thou thy harvest fruits?
Keep within thee the sweets of thy sustenance.

And thou, vine, why further dost thou give thy wine;
For an offering will not again be made therefrom in Zion.
Nor will first-fruits again be offered.

And do ye, O heavens, withhold your dew,
And open not the treasuries of rain:
And do thou, O sun, withhold the light of thy rays.

And do thou, O moon, extinguish the multitude of thy light;
For why should light rise again
Where the light of Zion is darkened?

And you, ye bridegrooms, enter not in.
And let not the brides adorn themselves with garlands;
And, ye women, pray not that ye may bear.

For the barren shall above all rejoice,
And those who have no sons shall be glad,
For those who have sons shall have anguish.

For why should they bear in pain,
Only to bury in grief?
Or why, again, should mankind have sons?

Or why should the seed of their kind again be named,
Where this mother is desolate,
And her sons are led into captivity?

From this time forward speak not of beauty,
And discourse not of gracefulness.

Moreover, ye priests, take ye the keys of the sanctuary,
And cast them into the height of heaven,
And give them to the Lord and say:

"Guard Thy house Thyself,
For lo! we are found false stewards."

And you, ye virgins; who weave fine linen
And silk with gold of Ophir,
Take with haste all [these] things
And cast [them] into the fire,
That it may bear them to Him who made them,
And the flame send them to Him who created them,
Lest the enemy get possession of them.

Moreover, I, Baruch, say this against thee, Babylon:
"If thou hadst prospered,
And Zion had dwelt in her glory,
Yet the grief to us had been great
That thou shouldst be equal to Zion.

But now, lo! the grief is infinite,
And the lamentation measureless,
For lo! thou art prospered
And Zion desolate.

Who will be judge regarding these things?
Or to whom shall we complain regarding that which has befallen
    us?
O Lord, how hast Thou born [it]?

Our fathers went to rest without grief,
And lo! the righteous sleep in the earth in tranquility.
For they knew not this anguish,
Nor yet had they heard of that which had befallen us.

Would that thou hadst ears, O earth,
And that thou hadst a heart, O dust:
That ye might go and announce in Sheol,
And say to the dead:
"Blessed are ye more than we who live."

[2 Baruch 10:5–11:7 (Charles 2:485–87)]

A still more profound expression of the prevailing perplexity comes
from 4 Ezra's reflection on the condition of the human being, now
shown, in its awful, terrible essence, to be a mass of contradictions.
Charlesworth introduces 4 Ezra as follows:

The pseudepigraphon was composed in the last decades of the
first century A.D., perhaps in Palestine. The original language is
Semitic, but it is difficult to decide whether it is Hebrew or Aramaic.
Most scholars now affirm the structural unity of the Jewish core,
chapters 3–14.

Eventually added to the core were two later Christian composi-
tions in Greek, now sometimes called 5 (chaps. 1–2), and 6 Ezra
(chaps. 15–16). The central section contains seven revelations to
Ezra, called Salathiel, by Uriel, in which *inter alia* the writer
confronts the problem of theodicy, and speculates about the coming
of the Messiah and the end of this age. The prefixed chapters,
probably added in the second century, delineate God's faithfulness
and Israel's apostasy with subsequent exhortations. The suffixed
chapters, probably added in the third century, contain prophecies of
woe, followed by exhortations and promises of deliverance for the
elect. [Charlesworth, *Research,* p. 112]

The complex of Pseudepigraphic writings in the name of Ezra affirms positions which the framers of the Mishnah may be assumed also to have maintained, for example, that God's ways are inscrutable, human intelligence is finite, and God loves Israel eternally (Box, in Charles 2:554–55). God is one, creator, judge, and redeemer of Israel and of the world. The Torah is the truth. These and also other positions, which Mishnah's philosophers may have received only with difficulty, if at all, are expressed in a series of colloquies and visions. Ezra speaks to God and engages in long discourses, as well as prayers. The angel talks back to Ezra so that the Pseudepigraph gives the impression of a philosophical dialogue, in mythic guise. Attention focuses upon the end which is coming, signs which precede the end. Subject to detailed attention is the divine plan for the world, the generations which follow one another under God's judgment. The earth now has grown old, and nature is degenerate. People are shorter than their parents. These are signs of the last time and the end. The road to future happiness is not going to be easy. There will be a Messiah, who will reign for four hundred years, then die. This catastrophe, however, will be followed by a general resurrection of the dead, final judgment, and the Day of Judgment. Only a few will make it through the suffering at the end. The Pseudepigraph is rich in prayers, visions, soliloquies and colloguies, conversations between angels and the speaker, and other dramatic artifices, but visions are what predominate, and conversations between the speaker and Heaven fill the work.

In 4 Ezra 7:62–74 the problem is phrased of human intelligence. The condition of the human being, of Adam, from creation to the age of destruction is natural. Catastrophe is the norm. For the very character of the human condition makes inevitable precisely what has happened even now. An extended quotation will serve us well when we consider what the framers of the Mishnah had to say in the same context:

> And I answered and said: O thou Earth, what has thou brought forth, if the mind is sprung from the dust as every other created thing! It had been better if the dust itself had even been unborn, that the mind might not have come into being from it.
>
> But, as it is, the mind grows with us, and on this account we are tormented, because we perish and know it.
>
> Let the human race lament,
>> but the beasts of the field be glad!
>
> Let all the earth-born mourn,
>> but let the cattle and flocks rejoice!
>
> For it is far better with them than with us; for they have no judgment to look for, neither do they know of any torture or of any salvation promised to them after death.

For what doth it profit us that we shall be preserved alive, but yet suffer great torment?
For all the earth-born
   are defiled with iniquities,
      full of sins,
      laden with offences.
And if after death we were not to come into judgment, it might, perhance, have been far better for us!
And he answered me and said: When the Most High made the world, and Adam, and all that came of him, he first prepared the Judgement, and the things that pertain unto the Judgement.
But, now, from thine own words understand: for thou hast said that the mind grows with us.
For this reason, therefore, shall the sojourners in the earth suffer torture, because having understanding, they yet wrought iniquity, and receiving precepts, they yet kept them not, and having obtained the Law, they set at naught that which they received.
What, then, will they have to say in the Judgement, or how shall they answer in the last times?
For how long a time hath the Most High been longsuffering with the inhabitants of the world—not for their sakes, indeed, but for the sake of the times which he has ordained!

[4 Ezra 7:62–74 (Box, in Charles 580)]

The materials of 4 Ezra (9:38–10:24) also encompass the recent events of Jerusalem and the Temple. The author phrases matters just as does the writer of 2 Baruch. This final, sizable quotation is apt because it asks the urgent questions of the age:

How is Sion, the mother of us all, in great grief and deep affliction? It is right now to mourn, seeing that we all mourn, and to grieve, seeing that we are all grief-stricken; thou, however, art grief-stricken for one son. But ask the earth, and she shall tell thee, that it is she who ought to mourn the fall of so many that have sprung into being upon her. Yea, from the beginning all who have been born, and others who are to come—lo! they go almost into perdition, and the multitude of them comes to destruction. Who, then, should mourn the more? Ought not she that has lost so great a multitude? or thou who grievest but for one? But if thou sayest to me: my lamentation is not like the earth's, for I have lost the fruit of my womb
   which I bare with pains
      and brought forth with sorrows—
but as regards the earth, (it is) according to the course of nature; the multitude present in it is gone as it came: then I say to thee: Just as thou hast borne (offspring) with sorrow, even so also the earth has borne (given) her fruit, namely man, from the beginning unto him that made her.

Now, therefore, keep thy sorrow within
  and bear gallantly the misfortunes that have befallen thee
For if thou wilt acknowledge God's decree to be just, thou shalt
receive thy son again in (due) time, and shalt be praised among
women. Therefore go into the city to thy husband. And she said
unto me: I will not do so: I will not enter the city, but here will I die.
So I proceeded to speak further unto her, and said: No, woman! no,
woman! do not do so;
      but suffer thyself to be prevailed upon by reason of
      Sion's misfortunes,
        be consoled by reason of Jerusalem's sorrow.
For thou seest how
  our sanctuary is laid waste,
      our altar thrown down;
  our Temple destroyed,
      our harp laid low;
  our song is silenced,
      our rejoicing ceased;
    the light of our lamp is extinguished,
      the ark of our covenant spoiled;
    our holy things are defiled,
      the name that is called upon us is profaned;
  our nobles are dishonored,
      our priests burnt,
  our Levites gone into captivity;
  our virgins are defiled,
      our wives ravished;
  our righteous are seized,
  [our saints are scattered,]
      our children are cast out,
      our heroes made powerless:
  and, what is more than all—
      Sion's seal now is sealed up dishonored,
      and given up into the hands of them that hate us.
Do thou, then, shake off thy great grief,
    abandon thy much sorrow,
That the Mighty One may again forgive thee,
    and the Most High give thee rest,
    a respite from thy troubles!

[4 Ezra 9:38–10:24 (Box, in Charles 2:603–5)]

The question of the age thus is framed in terms of Israel's condition.
The Temple, the location and model of creation, had been Israel's
heart and center. The world was made for the sake of Israel. Now
Israel had lost the Temple, creation had been deprived of its model.
The seven days of creation rehearsed, the apocalypse asks the inescap-
able and compelling question: How to bear it all, endure, and go on?

These extended quotations from Baruch and Ezra serve to set the stage for what is to come: a document, formed in the same context, which resorts to a completely different mode of expression to express an utterly unrelated message. Indeed, without this sizable excursus into the poetry of the apocalyptic writers, we should not have a clear picture of how different the Mishnah is from other books of the same period. Nor should we perceive so clearly how remarkable is the Mishnah's utter silence on those tremendous issues of suffering and atonement, catastrophe and apocalypse, expressed with such power in the passages just now cited at length.

Choices Made by Others

As I said, we make better sense of what people did do when we know what they chose not to do. This perspective on the people behind the Mishnah emerges from a consideration of the principal issues confronting all Israelites in the same place and time, the Land of Israel in the first and second centuries of the Common Era, and a review of the responses of people besides those represented in the Mishnah to those ubiquitous issues. For it is clear that the histories of several different kinds of Judaism run together through the period of time under discussion. But each of those histories follows its own course and its own path. This is natural, for the various people who made those histories, whose imagination and mode of being are expressed therein, all went their own way, ignoring one another, pretending to constitute, each for himself, the whole of the Israelite world—as indeed, in mind, was so.

The Mishnah represents one such world, an account of the world view and way of organizing and defining society, government and politics, time, space, the natural and sacred economy, the movement from birth to death, the formation of family and the dissolution of marriage—the entire way of life of the community to whom the document is addressed. What the Mishnah does not say, we shall see in ample detail, also contains a vivid statement on issues of the day. As a self-contained document, the Mishnah designs a whole world of meaning. But in its age were other such world-constructing systems for Israel.

Now when we turn to 2 Baruch and 4 Ezra, two other documents of this period, out of which an account of a different variety of Judaism in the earlier part of the time under study may be framed, we confront a quite different set of concerns. While as we shall see, the Mishnah's framers wished to talk about constructing a world, with detailed attention to economy and cult, the interplay between the sacred and the ordinary, the visionaries represented in the two great post-70 apocalypses lament a world now in ruins. On the surface the philosophers of the Mishnah speak about different things to different people. Yet the philosophers of the Mishnah live in the same ages as the poets of the apocalyptic writings. In that age none could for one minute avoid the definitive fact that the Temple had been destroyed. Since the mode of organizing life around the Temple and its cult was by then more than a thousand years old, the simple fact of its destruction drew attention and required response from whoever proposed to address the age beyond.

To be sure, there are important differences between the character of the Mishnah in its world, and the apocalyptic visions in theirs. While the Mishnah stands at the beginning of a movement of massive proportions and unlimited influence in the history of Judaism, 2 Baruch and 4 Ezra turn out to come at the end of another such movement. The Mishnah serves as a reference point to nearly all extant evidence in the succession to follow for many centuries. But the Mishnah on its part refers backward only to Scripture. It represents itself as an independent force in the history of Judaism. It demonstrably generates other forces. It is uncontingent in itself, but it makes other significant evidences and expressions of its variety of Judaism contingent upon it. For their part, 2 Baruch and 4 Ezra begin nothing and define nothing, but end much that is familiar. They find a comfortable position in a long sequence of equivalent documents. They take up long-explored and well-established themes. In response to the unprecedented events of their own day, they say no more and no less than had been said by others for a very long time, more than five hundred years. They serve to exemplify their type of Judaism. That is why our consideration of "apocalyptic Judaism" must be kept in mind as we turn to the Mishnah.

We move now from the writings infused with spiritual power to touch us directly and move us deeply, to rules of which we can scarcely make sense. The transition, to be appropriate, must be abrupt. There is no bridge, none of common sense, none of sensibility, from the poetry of suffering, hope, and despair, to the filigreed work of a rigidly patterned way of life. The Mishnah may be shown to be a kind of philosophy. It is not poetry. It may be demonstrated to be a response to a common set of concerns for creation and revelation and redemption. But it does not speak of these things, or, indeed, about any thing to which, after two thousand years, we may gain ready access or convenient entry.

2

THE MISHNAH'S JUDAISM
BEFORE 70

In the Beginning

The Mishnah reached completion and closure at about 200. It attributes
many sayings and ideas, however, to people who lived during the two
hundred years before that time. Some of these sayings contain ideas
which may be demonstrated to have been held in the earlier stages of
the formation of the larger body of ideas and laws now represented in
the Mishnah itself. When we gather these representations of what
people before 70 contributed to the stream of thought and reflection
ultimately flowing into the Mishnah, they do not form a sizable or
cogent set of beliefs and teachings. But they also are not random.
What we have is less than a system, but something more than a totally
disjointed set of mere facts. Still, what follows in this chapter and the
next must appear to be disjointed and arcane: an account of opinions
on scarcely coherent questions, a picture of random blips on a screeen
with asymmetrical and out-of-focus grids of depth and breadth. For
the period under discussion the evidence of the Mishnah testifies to
the state of opinion upon a few small matters. But from these few
facts—that one group took an exactly opposed position from another
on an issue no one else appears to have discussed at all—much can be
learned. The handful of facts in our hands serve like stones and sherds
in the hands of a dirt archeologist and like the report of marriage
taboos in the mind of an anthropologist. To be sure, even a rapid
survey of these fundamental data is apt to tax the reader's patience,
and rightly so. Without extended repetition of the facts of Scripture,
particularly the Mosaic codes of Exodus, Leviticus, Numbers, and
Deuteronomy, most of the issues of the Mishnah's law will be pure
gibberish, and, consequently, we shall know opinions on matters of
neither sense nor consequence.

But even if we understand those traces of expansion and signs of
fresh perspective yielded by a grasp of the details of the opinions held
before the wars, our work has scarcely begun. For understanding the
technical points of law hardly leads to a grasp of the state of people's
thought: what they proposed to express through these details, the
statement they wished to make. In this regard the contrast to the
readily accessible works of imagination—the visions, symbols, in-
vented transcendental discouse—of 2 Baruch and 4 Ezra is stunning.
Without much mediation or explanation, just now we found ourselves
able to grasp the sense of, and even respond to, the humanity of a cry
to earth no longer to produce its fruit. That is why it made sense to
quote at length. The world view centered upon coming redemption,
with its imagery of swords and its sounds of the clashing of shields,
fills the eye and ear with intelligible perception and even familiar
emotion. And this is as it should be. The messianic fervor of the first
century and the antimessianic despair of the second—the former
expecting too much, the latter hoping too little and too late—affected
the mass of Jews in the Israelite Land of the day. The Mishnah is
ahistorical, unpictorial, atactile, aniconic, and unemotional. It is abstract and intellectual. The philosophical exercise of forming a sensible
way of life in a stable, dependable community did not reach, let alone
touch, many people. It took a long time before ordinary Jews accepted
the measured, disciplined, and moderate system created in the centuries under study and collected and presented in the measured and
disciplined language of the Mishnah itself. The framers of the Mishnah
never lived to see that day.

So if the extreme sentiments of apocalypse and later on Gnosticism
prove readily accessible to us, it is because in their own day they also
reached and shaped the hearts of many. But then or now, how many
minds are there, to begin with, to be shaped? And how many wish it?
So, in sum, before us is the vision of philosophers, an intellectual
minority in a society prepared to move and wanting to be moved. In
their trivial discourse on questions the answer to which no one but
them really pursued, that vision is hidden and revealed. Before us lie
the beginnings of work which in its late day phrased in exquisitely
trivial terms some of those old, perennial issues of philosophy contemplated by Aristotle and later considered by the Stoics, issues of
potentiality and actuality, the physics of mixtures, and other odd and,
from a practical viewpoint, empty questions, the answers to which, as
I said, interested only those who asked the questions. In the end we
shall confront a work of absolute fantasy: a nonexistent Temple, fully
laid out, building, protocol, procedures; a society stretched out from
the walls of the Temple, with its space and its regulation of time, its
mode of establishing families and dissolving them, its economic life,

all proportioned in relationship to that imagined Temple and its imaginary cult. Fantasy? Yes, for the Temple then lay in ruins, and Jerusalem was a forbidden city for Israelites. The Mishnah replaces both with utopia. Before us at the end will emerge a city of the mind, particular place, framed in all due locative dimensions and requisite spatial descriptions, which, in fact, existed nowhere but in the mind, which by nature is utopian. Why therefore should we expect the concrete raw material of such a fantastic mental conjuration—a never-never land—to prove of ready accesss to us, when it was not self-evident in the minds of the people before whom, to begin with, the materials were laid forth? And, given the extraordinary mastery of the Mosaic law exhibited by the philosophers of the Mishnah, from beginning to closure, we hardly may take for granted that what to them appeared obvious, indeed self-evident, to us will be possessed of even crude significance.

Just as we quickly surveyed some representative and suggestive writings of apocalypse in response to the two wars so now, equally quickly, but in somewhat gerater differentiation of detail, we do the same. We now turn to that evidence which has awaited so long for this many-sided introduction and apology. We come to the Mishnah itself.

The Mishnah lays out its materials in six principal Divisions, each divided into tractates, arranged for the most part from largest in size to smallest. Even an account of the several stages in the unfolding of the Mishnah's law must survey that law in accord with the Mishnah's own mode of organizing it. This approach allows systematic attention to the several units of thought, in accord with their familiar setting and arrangement.

Here and in the next chapter we shall stand back and describe the conglomerate of rules and conceptions as these unfolded. In chapter 5 we survey the whole system. We shall in the end have three pictures of the formation of Judaism: the way matters stood before 70 (chapter 2), then the manner in which the laws coalesce before the war of 130 (chapter 3), and, finally, the entire and complete, fully formed system of the Mishnah as a whole, in 200 (chapter 5).

What we shall see in the end is that the Mishnah takes shape in a twofold process. Once a theme is introduced early in the history of law, it will be taken up and refined later on. Also, in the second and third stages in the formation of the Mishnah, many new themes with their problems emerge. These then are without precedent in the antecedent thematic heritage. The common foundations for the whole always are Scripture, of course, so that I may present a simple architectural simile. The Mishnah is like a completed construction of scaffolding. The foundation is a single plane, the Scriptures. The top platform also is a single plane, the Mishnah itself. But the infrastruc-

ture is differentiated. Underneath one part of the upper platform will
be several lower platforms, so that the supporting poles and pillars
reach down to intervening platforms; only the bottom platform rests
upon pillars set in the foundation. Yet another part of the upper
platform rests upon pillars and poles stretching straight down to the
foundation, without intervening platforms at all. So viewed from
above, the uppermost platform of the scaffolding forms a single,
uniform, and even plane. That is the Mishnah as we have it, six
Divisions, sixty-three tractates, five hundred thirty-one chapters. But
viewed from the side, that is, from the perspective of analysis, there is
much differentiation, so that, from one side, the upper platform rises
from a second, intermediate one, and, in places, from even a third,
lowest one. And yet, as I said, some of the pillars reach directly down
to the bedrock foundations.

To reveal the result at the outset: what is new in the period beyond
the wars is that part of the ultimate plane—the Mishnah as a whole—
which in fact rests upon the foundations not of antecedent thought but
of Scripture alone. What is basic in the period before the two wars is
the formation of that part of the Mishnah which sustains yet a second
and even a third layer of platform construction. What emerges between
the two wars, of course, will both form a plane with what comes
before, that platform at the second level, and yet will also lay foundations for a level above itself. But this intermediate platform also will
come to an end, yielding that space filled only by the pillars stretching
from Scripture on upward to the ultimate plane of the Mishnah's
completed and whole system. So let me now describe what I believe
to be the state of the law as a whole before 70.

The First Stage

The Mishnah as we know it originated in its Division of Purities. The
striking fact is that the Sixth Division is the only Division that yields a
complete and whole statement of a topic dating from before the wars
and its principal parts: (1) what imparts uncleanness; (2) which kinds
of objects and substances may be unclean; and (3) how these objects
or substances may regain the status of cleanness. Joined to episodic
rulings elsewhere, the principal parts of the Sixth Divison speak, in
particular, of cleanness of meals, food and drink, pots and pans. It
then would appear that the ideas ultimately expressed in the Mishnah
began among people who had a special interest in observing cultic
cleanness. There can be no doubt, moreover, that the context for such
cleanness is the home, not solely the Temple. The issues of the law
leave no doubt on that score. Since priests ate heave offering at home,

and did so in a state of cleanness, it was a small step to apply the same taboos to food which was not a consecrated gift to the priests. It is less clear whether we hear ideas solely of radical priests, who wish to eat their home meals in the same conditions of cultic cleanness which pertain to their meals in the Temple, or whether in addition there were lay people who wished to pretend they were priests by adopting for their ordinary meals at home the priests' taboos, originating in the cultic setting. I believe that the system began among radical priests joined by lay people to form a holiness sect, but that is just a guess.

In either case what is said through the keeping of these laws is that the food eaten at home, not deriving from the altar and its provision for the priesthood of meat not burned up in the fire, was as holy as the meal offerings, meat offerings, and drink offerings, consecrated by being set aside for the altar and then, in due course, partly given to the priests and partly tossed on the altar and burned up. If food not consecrated for the altar, not protected in a state of cleanness (in the case of wheat), or carefully inspected for blemishes (in the case of beasts), and not eaten by priests in the Temple, was deemed subject to the same restrictions as food consecrated for the altar, this carries implications about the character of that food, those who were to eat it, and the conditions in which it was grown. First, all food, not only that for the altar, was to be protected in a state of holiness, that is, separateness. Second, the place, the Land, in which the food was grown and kept was holy, just like the Temple. Third, the people, Israel, who were to eat that food were holy, just like the priesthood, in rank behind the Temple's chief caste. Fourth, the act of eating food anywhere in the Holy Land was analogous to the act of eating food in the Temple, by the altar.

All of these obvious inferences from the repertoire of laws on cleanness point to a profound conviction about the Land, people, produce, condition, and context of nourishment. The setting was holy. The actors were holy. And what, specifically, they did which had to be protected in holiness was eating. For when they ate their food at home, they ate it the way priests did in the Temple. And the way priests ate their food in the Temple, that is, the cultic rules and conditions observed in that setting, was like the way God ate his food in the Temple. That is to say, God's food and locus of nourishment were to be protected from the same sources of danger and contamination, preserved in the same exalted condition of sanctification (see Levine). So by acting, that is, eating, like God, Israel became like God: a pure and perfect incarnation, on earth in the Land which was holy, of the model of heaven. Eating food was the critical act and occasion, just as the priestly authors of Leviticus and Numbers had maintained when they made laws governing slaughtering beasts and burning up their flesh, baking pancakes and cookies with and without olive oil and burning them on the altar, pressing grapes and making wine and pouring it out onto the altar. The nourishment of the Land—meat, grain, oil, and wine—was set before God and burned ("offered up") in conditions of perfect cultic antisepsis.

In context this antisepsis provided protection against things deemed the opposite of nourishment, the quintessence of death: corpse matter, people who looked like corpses (Lev. 13), dead creeping things, blood when not flowing in the veins of the living, such as menstrual blood (Lev. 15), other sorts of flux (semen in men, nonmenstrual blood in women) which yield not life but then its opposite, so death. What these excrescences have in common, of course, is that they are ambivalent. Why? Because they may be one thing or the other. Blood in the living is the soul; blood not in the living is the soul of contamination. The corpse was once a living person, like God; the person with skin like a corpse's and who looks dead was once a person who looked alive; the flux of the *zab* (Lev. 15) comes from the flaccid penis, which under the right circumstances, that is, properly erect, produces semen and makes life. What is at the margin between life and death and can go either way is what is the source of uncleanness. But, as we shall see, that is insufficient. For the opposite, in the priestly code, of *unclean* is not only *clean*, but also *holy*. The antonym is not to be missed: death or life, unclean or holy.

So the cult is the point of struggle between the forces of life and nourishment and the forces of death and extinction: meat, grain, oil, and wine, against corpse matter, dead creeping things, blood in the wrong setting, semen in the wrong context, and the like. Then, on the occasions when meat was eaten, mainly, at the time of festivals or other moments at which sin offerings and peace offerings were made, people who wished to live ate their meat, and at all times ate the staples of wine, oil, and bread, in a state of life and so generated life. They kept their food and themselves away from the state of death as much as possible. And this heightened reality pertained at home, as much as in the Temple, where most rarely went on ordinary days. The Temple was the font of life, the bulwark against death.

In this statement of the convictions of the priestly code about the metaphysical meaning of cultic cleanness and taboos relevant thereto, we see why Israelites interested in rules about meals will have thought such rules, in particular, to be important. It is hardly surprising, once the meal became a focus of attention, that the other two categories of the law which I believe yield principles or laws deriving from the period before the wars present precisely the same sorts of rules. Laws on growing and preparing food will attract attention as soon as people wish to speak, to begin with, about how meals are to be eaten (cf.

Wächter; Dombrowski). That accounts for the obviously lively interest in the biblical taboos of agriculture. Since, further, meals are acts of society, they call together a group. Outside of the family, the natural unit, such a group will be special, cultic. If a group is going to get together, it will be on a Sabbath or festival, not on a workday. So laws governing the making of meals on those appointed times will inevitably receive attention. Nor is it surprising that, in so far as there are any rules pertinent to the cult, they will involve those aspects of the cult which apply also outside of the cult, that is, how a beast is slaughtered, rules governing the disposition of animals of a special status (e.g., firstborn), and the like.

That the rules for meals pertain not to isolated families but to a larger group is strongly suggested by the other area which evidently was subjected to sustained attention before the wars, I mean, laws governing who may marry whom. The context in which the sayings assigned to the authorities before the wars are shaped is the life of a small group of people, defining its life apart from the larger Israelite society while maintaining itself wholly within that society. Three points of ordinary life formed the focus for concrete, social differentiation: food, sex, and marriage. What people ate, how they conducted their sexual lives, and whom they married or to whom they gave their children in marriage would define the social parameters of their group. These facts indicate who was kept within the bounds, and who was excluded and systematically maintained at a distance. For these are the things—the only things—subject to the independent control of the small group. The people behind the laws, after all, could not tell other people than their associates what to eat or whom to marry. But they could make their own decisions on these important, but humble, matters. By making those decisions in one way and not in some other, they moreover could keep outsiders at a distance and those who to begin with adhered to the group within bounds. Without political control, they could not govern the transfer of property or other matters of public interest. But without political power, they could and did govern the transfer of their women. It was in that intimate aspect of life that they thereby firmly established the outer boundary of their collective existence. The very existence of the group and the concrete expression of its life, therefore, comes under discussion in the transfer of women.

The Laws as a Whole

It seems to me no accident at all that those strata of Mishnaic law which appear to go back to the period before the wars deal specifically

with the special laws of marriage, distinctive rules on when sexual
relations may and may not take place, and the laws covering the
definition of sources of uncleanness and the attainment of cleanness,
with specific reference to domestic meals. Nor is it surprising that for
the conduct of the cult and the sacrificial system, about which the
group may have had its own doctrines but over which it neither
exercised control nor even aspired to exercise control, there appears
to be no systemic content or development whatsoever.

To recapitulate the argument: once the group takes shape around
some distinctive, public issue or doctrine, as in odd taboos about
eating, it also must take up the modes of social differentiation which
will ensure the group's continued existence. For the group, once it
comes into being, has to aspire to define and shape the ordinary lives
of its adherents and to form a community expressive of its larger world
view. The foundations of an enduring community will then be laid
down through rules governing what food may be eaten, under what
circumstances, and with what sort of people; whom one may marry
and what families may be joined in marriage; and how sexual relationships are timed. Indeed, to the measure that these rules not only differ
from those observed by others but in some aspect or other render the
people who keep them unacceptable to those who do not, as much as,
to the sect, those who do not keep them are unacceptable to those who
do, the lines of difference and distinctive structure will be all the more
inviolable.

The Mishnah before the wars begins its life among a group of people
who are joined together by a common conviction about the eating of
food under ordinary circumstances in accord with cultic rules to begin
with applicable, in the mind of the priestly lawyers of Leviticus and
Numbers, to the Temple alone. This group, moreover, had other rules
which affected who might join and who might not. As I said, these
laws formed a protective boundary, keeping in those who were in,
keeping out those who were not. In accord with the inductive principles which guide this account of the unfolding of the Mishnah, if we
wish to identify the social group in which the Mishnah originated, it is
at this point that discourse must come to a conclusion. The reason is
that the Mishnah does not tell us the name of the group represented by
the names of Shammai and Hillel and their Houses, Gamaliel, Simeon
b. Gamaliel, his son, and others who appear in the Mishnah and who
clearly form the earliest stratum of its named authorities. More important: the convictions of the named authorities deal with details. The
vast territories of agreement have not been surveyed and marked out
by them in particular. So, for all we know, the concrete matters subject
to dispute represent the points at issue of no more than a tiny sector

of a much larger group, which, in other ways, will have had still other points of discourse and contention.

The upshot is simple. We know of two particular groups in the period before the wars who held significant convictions about taboos governing meals and about marriage into their groups, the Essenes and the Pharisees. Because Gamaliel and his son, Simeon, appear in the Mishnah and, when they appear in other writings (Acts 5:34; Josephus, *Life,* 190–94), also are called Pharisees, people generally assume that the book which contains sayings in their names is their book, that is, a book originating among Pharisees. So it is assumed that the Mishnah is a Pharisaic book. While that may well be so, the internal evidence of the Mishnah itself does not direct our attention only to the Pharisees. As I just said, there were, after all, Essenes who can have kept these same laws within their social framework. And much which is written about the Pharisees does not appear to describe a holiness sect or an eating club at all. Nor does the Mishnah even mention Pharisees in those pericopes the ideas of which can securely be shown to belong to the period before the wars (see Lightstone, *Sadducees*). The Mishnah speaks mostly about the Houses of Shammai and Hillel. As I pointed out, we do not even know whether before us are the ideas only of radical priests, or only of lay people pretending to be priests, or of a mixture of the two. The information on the Essenes suggests the third of the three possibilities. But that does not settle the question for the group behind the stratum of the Mishnah set before the wars. And, it is clear, we are not even sure we can call the group by any name more specific and definitive than *group,* for instance, a *sect.* We use general language so as not to invoke the meanings asssociated with more particular categories.

What demands attention, rather, is a different question. Why should the Temple and the ideas of its priests have played so important a role in the mind of the people (whoever they were) who are represented by the earliest layer of ideas ultimately contained in the Mishnah? Since, as we shall see time and again, what the Mishnah presents is nothing other than what the Scripture says, and Scriptures that are chosen for representation time and again are those in the priestly code, we have to wonder why the priestly themes and repertoire of concerns should have so occupied the imagination and fantasy of the people who formed the group (or groups) represented in the laws before us. It is the continuity from the priestly code of the seventh through the fifth century B.C. to the beginnings of the Mishnaic code of the first and second centuries A.D., which requires explanation. For, end as much as beginning, the Mishnah is the formation of the priestly perspective on the condition of Israel (see below, pp. 94–96).

The Mishnah states what priests had long said, but in other language, in other documents. True, the Mishnah has its own perspective and method. These are drastically different from those of the priestly code. As we shall see, the Mishnah employs the list-making method of the scribes. Indeed, the Mishnah takes up a remarkably unfriendly position on the priesthood, while acknowledging and affirming every single right and benefit owing to the priesthood. So, in sum, the Mishnah is not a merely contingent and secondary development of what is in the priestly code. Nonetheless, the continuity from the priestly code to the Mishnah is firm and impressive. If the founders of the Mishnaic code had something distinctive to say, it was in the vocabulary and images of the priestly code. The words were their own. But the deep syntax of the sacred, the metaphysical grammar, belong to the priesthood from olden times. That is why it now becomes urgent to speculate on why the priestly code should have exercised so profound and formative an influence upon the founders and first framers of Mishnaic law.

From the Priestly Code to the Beginning of the Mishnaic Code

The reason that the priestly code (P) (Lev. 1–15) exercised the formative power it did is that the problems addressed and (for some) solved in the priestly code remained chronic long after the period of its formation, from the seventh century onward down to its closure in the time of Ezra and Nehemiah. True, there were many ways to confront and cope with the problems I shall specify. After all, third and fourth Isaiahs flourished in the same time as did the philosophers, storytellers, and lawyers whose ideas ultimately come to a single formation and to closure in P. Jeremiah and the writers and editors of Deuteronomy were contemporaries too. But the priestly code states a powerful answer to a pressing and urgent question. Since, as I shall now suggest, that question would remain a perplexity continuing to trouble Israelites for a long time, it is not surprising that the priestly answer to it, so profound and fundamental in its character, should for its part have continued to attract and impress people too.

That is the argument I wish now to lay out. In order to follow it, we have first to locate ourselves in the time of closure of the priestly code, that is, in the late sixth and fifth centuries B.C., and to specify the critical tensions of that period. Once we have seen the character of these tensions, without needing much exposition we shall realize that the same tensions persisted and confronted the thinkers whose reflection led to the conclusions, in resolution of those ongoing points of dissonance, that the Temple's holiness enveloped and surrounded Israel's Land and demarcated its people too (cf. Russell).

What marks ancient Israel as distinctive perenially is its preoccupation with defining itself. In one way or another Israel sought means of declaring itself distinct from its neighbors. The stress on exclusion of the neighbors from the group, and of the group from the neighbors, runs contrary to the situation of ancient Israel, with unmarked frontiers of culture, the constant giving and receiving among diverse groups, generally characteristic of ancient times. The persistent stress on differentiation, yielding a preoccupation with self-definition, also contradicts the facts of the matter. In the time of the formation of the priestly code, the people Israel was deeply affected by the shifts and changes in social and cultural and political life and institutions captured by the word "Hellenization." That was the case long before the conquest of Alexander. We may trace the ongoing preoccupation with self-definition to the context which yielded the later Scriptural legacy of the Pentateuchal redaction, for it was in that protracted moment of confusion and change that the priestly code came to closure, and with it, the Pentateuchal heritage. As Morton Smith shows (*Palestinian Parties*, pp. 57–81), the epoch of "Hellenization" began long before Alexander and continued long afterward. Greek military forces, Greek traders, Greek merchandise, and Greek ways penetrated the Land of Israel. There were substantial Greek settlements before Alexander's conquest. Greek influence thereafter intensified. Now as we know, it is in the time of Nehemiah and Ezra that the priestly writers brought to completion and closure the collection of cultic traditions we now know as P. And, as Smith amply demonstrates, Nehemiah himself is the archetype of a Greek *tyrannos,* a type Smith describes as follows: "These new rulers were products of the economic and social change which was taking place all over the area. . . . Barbarian invasions had destroyed the order of the more ancient world, brought trade almost to a standstill, and reduced much of the New East to a culture of mere local subsistence." As civilization began to recover, "stabilization of society led to increase in population and foreign trade. Foreign trade increased venture capital and also produced a class of new rich. . . . Increases of capital, or population, and consequently, of need, produced successively borrowing . . . default, confiscation, and enslavement. The resultant resentment and social instability were often used by ambitious political leaders to secure a following. . . . Such revolutionary leaders . . . were known as 'tyrants' " (*Palestinian Parties, p.* 138). Nehemiah was one of these types. One of the characteristic parts of the program of such a political figure was to pass measures, again in Smith's words, "such as public works programs, cancellation of debts, release of persons enslaved for debt, confiscation of the property of their wealthy opponents, and redistribution of land" (*Palestinian Parties, pp.* 138–39). The program of the *tyrannos* included codification of laws of a society as a (somewhat later) response to social development.

All of this political and legislative program therefore is part of the common inheritance of the modernization of the Middle East even prior to Alexander.

The upshot of the codification and closure of the law under Nehemiah was to produce a law code which laid heavy emphasis on the exclusivist character of the Israelite God and cult. "Judaism" gained the character of a cultically centered way of life and world view. Both rite and myth aimed at the continuing self-definition of Israel by separation from the rest of the world and exclusion of the rest of the world. Order against chaos meant holiness over uncleanness, life over death. The purpose was to define Israel against the background of the other peoples of the Near and Middle East, with whom Israel had much in common, and, especially, to differentiate Israel from its neighbors, e.g., Samaritans, in the same country. Acute differentiation was required in particular because the social and cultural facts were precisely to the contrary: common traits hardly bespeaking clear-cut points of difference, except of idiom. The mode of differentiation taken by the Torah literature in general, and the priestly sector of that literature in particular, was cultic. The meaning, however, also was social. The power of the Torah composed in this time lay in its control of the Temple. The Torah made that Temple the pivot and focus. The Torah literature, with its jealous God, who cares what people do about rather curious matters, and the Temple cult, with its total exclusion of the non-Israelite from participation, and (all the more so) from cultic comensality, raised high those walls of separation and underlined such distinctiveness as already existed. The life of Israel flowed from the altar; what made Israel Israel was the center, the altar.

Now we must consider that it was at just this time, from the seventh to the fifth century B.C., that the roads were opening to carry trade, culture, ideas, and, above all, to permit the mixing of peoples and races through what we may call direct personal encounter, that is, marriage (and parallel activities). So it was at just this time, long before the cultural reaction which expressed the oriental response to the political changes effected by Alexander and his successors (see Eddy), that groups had to take up and contemplate what made them different from one another. It also was clear at, or before, this time that a fair part of Israel would not live in "its own" Land at all. Israel also would preserve its distinctive group life and character somewhere else. That complicating fact also made all the more necessary a persistent exercise of self-definition—meaning, more accurately, self-differention—from the diverse people among whom, and essentially like whom, Israel lived out its life.

So long as Israel remained essentially within its own Land and frame of social reference, that is, before the conflagration of the sixth century

B.C., the issue of separation from neighbors could be treated casually. When the very core and heart of what made Israel into Israel were penetrated by the doubly desolating and disorienting experiences of both losing the Land and then coming back, by the exercises in confusion in economic and social relationships to which I have alluded, and by the fact that the Land to which Israelites returned in no way permitted contiguous and isolated Israelite settlement, then the issue of self-definition clearly would emerge. It would remain on the surface and chronic. And it would persist for the rest of Israelite history, from the return to Zion and the formation of the Torah literature even down to our own day. The reason for the persistence is that the social forces which lent urgency to the issue of who is Israel (or, later, of who is a Jew) would remain. It is hardly an exaggeration to say that this confusion about the distinctive and ongoing identification to be assigned to Israel would define the very framework of the social and imaginative ecology of the Jewish people (see Neusner, *Way*, pp. xi–xiv). So long as memory remained, the conflicting claims of exclusivist Torah literature and universalist prophecy, of a people living in utopia, in no particular place, while framing its vision to itself in the deeply locative symbols of cult and center—these conflicting claims would make vivid the abiding issue of self-definition.

Now when we confront the matter of the Mishnah's place in the ongoing issue of who is Israel, we must place the beginnings of the Mishnah into historical context. Otherwise we shall lose sight of what is important in the Mishnah's version of Israel's definition and miss the reason for its continuity with the priestly one. For the Mishnah at its origins carries forward precisely those priestly and cultic motifs which proved important at the first encounter, in the time of Ezra and Nehemiah, between Israel and what would be Israel's enduring ecological framework. That was the encounter between the pressing claim to be exclusive and to serve an exclusivist God, on the one side, and the equally paramount facts of diffuse settlement in trivial numbers and diverse locations, on the other. These and related political and social factors making for the very opposite of an exclusive and closed society within high borders created a dissonance, not ever resolved, between social facts and the fantastic self-perceptions of Israel. Indeed, the very stress of the Torah literature on maintaining high and inviolable frontiers around Israel bespeaks the very opposite: a porous border, an unmarked boundary, an open road from group to group, down which, as I said, not only ideas but also unions of people could and did travel.

3

THE TURN OF THE SECOND CENTURY: AGE OF ORDER AND HOPE

The Issues of the Age

The obvious and accessible dilemmas of Israel's suffering at the hand of gentiles, the deeper meaning of the age in which the Temple had been ruined and Israel defeated, the resort for expressing public sorrow to evocative symbols of private suffering and its mystery, the discourse on the meaning of human history in the light of this awful outcome for Israel—none of these (to us accessible and sympathetic) themes and modes of thought comes to the surface in those themes and topics which the precursors of the Mishnaic system deem the appropriate focus of discourse. It is as if before us in the Mishnah are bystanders, taken up with the result of the catastrophe and determined to make a quite distinctive statement about what was important in it. But the miserable world of the participants—the people who had fought, lost, and suffered—seems remote. It would stand to reason that before us is the framing of the issue of 70 by the priests, alongside people who, before the wars, had pretended to be priests and imitated their cultic routines. To such people as these, the paramount issues of 70 were issues of cult. The consequences demanding sustained attention, therefore were the effects of the wobbling of the pivot for the continued life of the cult in those vast stretches of the Israelite Land which remained holy, among those sizable Israelite populations of the country which remained vital. Israel had originally become Israel and sustained its perpetual vocation through its living on the holy Land and organizing all aspects of its holy life in relationship to the conduct of the holy Temple, eating like priests and farming in accord with the cultic taboos and obsessions with order and form, dividing up time between profane and holy in relationship to the cult's calendar and temporal division of its own rites. Now Israel remained Israel, loyal to its calling, through continuing to live in the mirror and under the aspect of that same cult. But these are matters which will require our attention to their own context. Let us now survey those laws which appear to have emerged in the age between the wars.

The Issues of the Law

The principal initiatives and propositions of the law after 70 prove to be either predictable on the basis of what had just now happened or wholly continuous with what had gone before. The point of interest in the catastrophe of the First War against Rome, for the people whose ideas came down to the framers of the Mishnah, therefore lies in the stunning facts that, first, the Temple building had been destroyed, and, second, the cult had come to a halt. To them these points of total disorientation and sociocultic disorganization formed the problematic of the age. At issue were not tragedy and catastrophic history, but the shaking of the foundations of orderly life. Needed was not poetry but order. To the founders of the Mishnah the aftermath of the first defeat brought to an end the orderly life of the villages and the Land, the reliable relationship of calendar and crop with cult. The problematic of the age therefore was located in that middle range of life between the personal tragedy of individuals, who live and die, and the national catastrophe of the history of Israel. The pivot had wobbled: everything organized around it and in relationship to it had quaked. Left out were those two things at the extremes of this middle world: private suffering, and national catastrophe in the context of history, the encompassing history of Israel and of the world alike. That is why, when we contemplate how others of the same time framed the issues of the day, we are struck by the contrast.

The sole fact to be adduced as definitive for the interpretation of materials attributed to authorities in the aftermath of the destruction of the Temple is that the Temple was destroyed. That fact by definition affected all else. But it also is general. There is no way to move from the self-evident facts that the Temple building was destroyed, the cult was no longer carried on, and the priesthood and Levites were now unemployed, to the specificities of the laws on these topics reliably assigned to the period under discussion. But there is no need to do so. For the main point of interest in an account of Judaism's unfolding is the expansion of the topics subject to discussion among precursors of the Mishnah's ultimate form, frame, and system. And, as we shall now

see, the two new themes brought under systematic discourse directly
relate to the destruction of the Temple, namely, laws affecting the
taxes paid to the class of the poor and the case of the priests, on the
one side, and laws governing the conduct of the cult itself, on the other
side. Since, moreover, the production of crops in accord with certain
taboos was intimately related to the life of the cult, the sustained
interest in the application of at least one significant taboo, that concerning mixed seeds, formed part of a larger statement about the way
in which the country would respond to the loss of the Temple. Matters
were to go forward as if the Temple still stood, because the Land
retained its holiness, and God, his title to, and ownership of, the Land.
Therefore the class of the poor, for its part, retained a right to a portion
of crops prior to the completion of their harvest, and the priesthood,
its claim to a part of them afterward. Sustained interest in the conduct
of the cult, of course, represented a similar act of hope, an expression
of the certainty that, just as God retained ownership of the Land, so
too Israel remained responsible to maintain knowledge of the proper
conduct of the sacrificial cult which returned to God part of what
belonged to God out of the herds and crops of the holy Land and
which so secured Israel's right to the rest. So far from the viewpoint
of the Mishnah's precursors, what required sustained reflection in the
aftermath of the destruction was the disorientation of the country's
cultic life, both in its conduct of the agricultural—that is, the economic—affairs, governed as they were by laws emanating from the cult
and meant to place economic life into relationship with the cult, and in
its performance of the cult itself. The profound disorientation of defeat
and destruction, the disorder brought about by the collapse of basic
institutions of government, culture, and faith—these form the crisis
defined in this particular way by these people.

Alongside these two fresh points of interest, the established one in
the conduct of a meal in conditions of cleanness enjoyed continued
interest. In addition to a close continuation of thinking already evi-
denced prior to the war, moreover, a number of new topics came up.

First, systematic attention was paid to sources of uncleanness
which, prior to the war, seem in legal thought to have been neglected.
That is, sources of uncleanness on which no work had been done in
organizing and amplifying laws now received sustained attention. Important here is significant and rigorous work on the unclean persons
and objects (houses, clothing) discussed at Lev. 13 and 14. These now
join the unclean persons and objects of Lev. 11, 12, and 15, to which
ample attention already had been paid.

Second, there was a quite original essay attempted on the one rite of
the cult which was performed outside of the Temple building itself,
namely, burning the red cow and mixing its ashes with spring water to

make purification water for persons affected by corpse uncleanness (Num. 19:1ff.). What is said in this essay, as it is worked out between the wars, is that a place of true cleanness can be formed outside of the Temple. (Whether or not the rite itself was carried on is not information provided by the Mishnah; in fact, we do not know.) What had to be done was situating the conduct of the rite outside the Temple in an appropriate relationship to the Temple itself. That is, determining whether or not the rite should be done precisely as rites were done in the Temple, or, in a mirror image, precisely the opposite of the way rites were done in the Temple, was the principal focus. This fundamental inquiry into the governing analogies generated ongoing exegesis. Through imposing on participants in the rite perfect attentiveness and perpetual concern for what they were doing while they were engaged in the rite, the law would make possible that state of cleanness appropriate to the conduct of a sacred rite in the otherwise unclean secular world. It would follow that a state of cleanness still higher than that of the Temple would be contemplated. The rules would demand remarkable attentiveness. Why all of this should come under discussion at just this time is obvious. For the underlying notion is continuous with that of the laws of Purities prior to 70, that is to say, cleanness outside of the Temple building *is* possible. A state of cleanness outside of the conduct of the Temple cult therefore may be required for certain purposes. What now is added thus is predictable, given what had been said before 70. Just as a meal can and should be eaten in a state of cultic cleanness by people not engaged in the eating of bread and meat originating as priestly gifts in the Temple, so it is possible even to conduct that one rite which Scripture itself deems legitimate when performed outside the "tent of meeting," the Temple. The laws remain valid; the relevant ones require study.

The Age of Transition

The destruction of the Temple is important, in the unfolding of the history of the Mishnah's laws and ideas, principally because of what it does not demarcate. It does not mark a significant turning in the history of the laws of Purities. These unfolded within the generative principles of their own logic. The inner tensions embedded from before 70 in the exercise of locating the unclean on a continuum with the holy and of situating ordinary food in place of that continuum account for what was said after 70. The loss of the Temple, enormous though it was, does not. The expectation that the rites governing agriculture and the disposition of the produce of the Land would remain valid accounts for the evidence we have surveyed, just as that same expectation, that people would eat in a state of cultic cleanness, clearly is in evidence in the character of the laws of Purities between the wars. True, the destruction of the Temple and the supposedly temporary cessation of the cult precipitated thought on laws governing the Temple altar and the priests in the act of sacrifice. That was a natural interest among people who, to begin with, thought that what happened in the Temple formed the center and focus of Israelite life. With the Temple gone, people will naturally have wondered whether some deep flaw in the conduct of its rites might explain the awful punishment Israel suffered in the destruction of the Temple and the holy city. So, in that same, essentially priestly, perspective of the world, it was entirely predictable that sustained thought on the right conduct of the cult should have gotten under way. So the themes and detailed principles collected in the Divisions of Agriculture, Holy Things, and Purities, the first and the third continuing from before the war, the second beginning in its aftermath, testify to a continuity of vision, a perpetuation of focus.

The people whose ideas come to full expression and closure in the Mishnah, as we shall see later on, were diverse. But in so far as the definition of the group is concerned, who, before and between the wars, contributed to the ultimate corpus of ideas contained in what was framed after the wars, that definition remains unchanged. They were priests and lay people who aspired to act like priests. These are the ones whose fantasy lies before us in the stratum of the laws of the Mishnah just now surveyed. Yet fresh elements in their thought turn out to have laid the foundations for what, in the end, is truly Mishnaic about the Mishnah, I mean, the Mishnah's message at its deepest structure about the interplay between sanctification, on the one side, and the human will, on the other. But that is something to which we shall return much later in this story.

Instead, we have to stand back from the laws we have surveyed and provide an overview of what was accomplished between the wars. That accomplishment may be stated very simply. The period between the wars marks a transition in the unfolding of the Mishnaic law and system. The law moved out of its narrow, sectarian framework. But it did not yet attain that full definition, serviceable for the governance of a whole society and the formation of a government for the nation as a whole, which would be realized in the aftermath of the wars. The marks of the former state remained. But those of the later character of the Mishnaic system began to make their appearance. Still, the systemic fulfillment of the law would be some time in coming. For, as I shall point out in the next section, the system as a whole in its ultimate shape would totally reframe the inherited vision. In the end the Mishnah's final framers would accomplish what was not done before or between the wars: make provision for the ordinary condition of

Israelite men and women, living everyday lives under their own government. The laws suitable for a sect would remain, to be joined by others which, in the aggregate, would wholly revise the character of the whole.

The shift would be from a perspective formed upon the Temple mount, to a vision framed within the plane of Israel, from a cultic to a communal conception, and from a center at the locative pivot of the altar, to a system resting upon the utopian character of the nation as a whole. To be sure, this still would be what the cult-centered vision had perceived: a holy nation in a holy Land living out a holy life and deriving sustenance from the source of life, through sanctification set apart from death and uncleanness. But the shift is made. The orbit moved to a path other than what it was. Between the wars the shift is yet to be discerned. But if the orbit was the same as it had been for well over half a millennium, still, we see a wobble in the pivot.

When we take up the changes in this transitional period, we notice, first of all, continuity with the immediate past. What was taking place after 70 is encapsulated in the expansion, along predictable and familiar lines, of the laws of uncleanness, so to these we turn first.

Continuities

If the destruction of Jerusalem and the Temple in 70 marks a watershed in the history of Judaism, the development of the system of uncleanness does not indicate it. The destruction of the Temple in no way interrupted the unfolding of those laws, consideration of which is well attested when the Temple was standing and the cult maintained. Development is continuous in a second aspect as well. We find that, in addition to carrying forward antecedent themes and supplying secondary and even tertiary conceptions, the authorities between the wars develop new areas and motifs of legislation. These turn out to be both wholly consonant with the familiar ones, and, while fresh, generated by logical tensions in what had gone before. If, therefore, the destruction of the Temple raised in some minds the question of whether the system of cleanness at home would collapse along with the cult, the rules and system before us in no way suggest so. To be sure, the destruction of the Temple does mark a new phase in the growth of the law. What now happens is an evidently rapid extension of the range of legislation, on the one side, and provision of specific and concrete rules for what matters of purity were apt to have been taken for granted but not given definition before 70, on the other. So the crisis of 70 in the system of uncleanness gives new impetus to movement along lines laid forth long before.

Let us first dwell upon the points of continuity, which are many and impressive. The development of the rules on the uncleanness of menstrual blood, the *zab,* and corpse uncleanness is wholly predictable on the basis of what has gone before. The principal conceptual traits carry forward established themes. For example, if we have in hand an interest in resolving matters of doubt, then, in the present age, further types of doubts will be investigated. Once we know that a valid birth is not accompanied by unclean blood, we ask about the definition of valid births. Rulings on corpse contamination dwell upon secondary and derivative issues. One new idea is the interest in projections from a house and how they too overshadow and so bring corpse uncleanness. It is from this point that an important development begins. Once we treat the tent as in some way functional, it is natural to focus upon the process or function of overshadowing in general. A major innovation in regard to tranfer of the contamination of corpse matter through the tent is the notion that the tent takes an active role, combining the diverse bits and pieces and corpse uncleanness into a volume sufficient to impart corpse uncleanness. What is done is to treat the overshadowing as a function, rather than the tent as a thing. Here the mode of thought is both contrastive and analogical.

Changes

What is new now requires attention. The comparison of the table in the home to the cult in the Temple is an old theme in the Mishnaic system. What is done at just this time appears to have been the recognition of two complementary sequences, the removes of uncleanness, the degrees of holiness. The former involves several steps of contamination from the original source of uncleanness. The latter speaks of several degrees of sanctification, ordinary food, heave offering, food deriving from the altar (holy things), and things involved in the preparation of purification water. Each of the latter is subject to the effects of contamination produced by each of the former, in an ascending ladder of sensitivity to uncleanness. Now this complex structure seems to me to result from the exceedingly difficult problem facing the Mishnaic system: what to do with the entire metaphor of domestic cleanness now that its cultic focus and center are (for the moment) no more. The answer is to treat the domestic table no longer as *like* the cult. The table now is a diminished cult, a lesser sanctuary, a place where the sacred abides, to be sure, not wholly as it did in the Temple. The metaphor of altar and hearth is shattered, but its pieces are put together into a not very different construction. When the table at home is deemed to be like the altar in the Temple, then we compare holy things to ordinary food and there is no reason to introduce the matter of heave offering. But when the table at home is placed into a continuum with the holy things of the cult, then what links the one to the other is precisely the continuing presence of the priesthood and its heave offering. So long as the priests preserve and eat heave offering in a state of cleanness, there is a way of relating the table at home to some higher sanctity, leading, moreover, to the highest. Once, therefore, the material and concrete continuum is worked out, it demands inclusion of attention to the one remaining material (nonmetaphorical) element of cultic sanctity, the priests' own food. That then completes the progression: the table of the ordinary Israelite, kept clean like the heave offering of the priesthood, points toward the ultimate sanctity inhering in the now-devastated altar. The steps in the ladder downward, to the corpse, then become possible, all forming a single continuum of death to life. This brilliant construction, created between the wars, is at its foundations continuous with what had gone before.

Treating as sufficient for the present purpose what was said above about the unfolding of agricultural laws between the wars (see p. 54), we turn directly to another area of the law closely linked to the themes and conceptions which already were well established, and yet, an essentially new topic for intense analysis, Holy Things. At issue now is the formation, between the wars, of laws governing the cult. The principal statement of this new system is as follows: the Temple is holy. Its priests therefore are indispensable. But the governance of the Temple now is to be in accord with Torah, and it is the sage who knows Torah and therefore applies it. Since a literal reading of Scripture prevented anyone's maintaining that someone apart from the priest could be like a priest and do the things priests do, it was the next best thing to impose the pretense that priests must obey laymen in the conduct even of the priestly liturgies and services. This is a natural next step in the development of the law. A second paramount trait of the version of the system between the wars is its rationalization of those uncontrolled powers inherent in the sacred cult as laid forth by Leviticus. The lessons of Nadab and Abihu and numerous other accounts of the cult's or altar's intrinsic *mana* (inclusive of the *herem*) are quietly set aside. The altar sanctifies what is appropriate to it, not whatever comes into contact with its power. It is not too much to say that, in that principle, the sacred is forced to conform to simple conceptions of logic and sense, its power uncontrollably to strike out dramatically reduced. This same rationality extends to the definition of the effective range of intention. If one intends to do improperly what is not in any event done at all, one's intention is null. Third, attention is paid to defining the sorts of offerings required in various situations of sin or guilt. Here too the message is not to be missed. Sin still is to be expiated, when circumstances permit, through the sacrificial system. Nothing has changed. There is no surrogate for sacrifice, an exceedingly important affirmation of the cult's continuing validity among people burdened with sin and aching for a mode of atonement. Finally, we observe that the established habit of thinking about gifts to be paid to the priest accounts for the choices of topics on fees paid to maintain the cult. All pertain to priestly gifts analogous to tithes and heave offerings. Tithe of cattle is an important subject to considerable development. The upshot is that the principal concerns of the Division of Holy Things are defined by the end of the age between the wars.

Episodic, but sometimes not unimportant, conceptions only later on to be ultimately fully developed in the Mishnah's other three Divisions, on Appointed Times, Women, and Damages, make an appearance. We shall now survey the state of thought on topics ultimately brought together in these three divisions of what was to be the system of the closed and completed Mishnah. Systematic work on the formation of a Division of Appointed Times did not get under way in the aftermath of the destruction of the Temple. The established interest in rules governing meals, however, was carried forward in laws reliably assigned to the time between the wars. There is some small tendency to develop laws pertinent to the observance of the Sabbath: a few of these laws were important and generated later developments. But the age between the wars may be characterized as a period between important developments. Work on legislation for meals on Sabbaths and festivals had begun earlier. The effort systematically and thoroughly to legislate for the generality of festivals, with special attention to conduct in the Temple cult, would begin later on. In the intervening generations only a little work was done, and this was not systematic.

Certainly there was ample reason now to legislate for the festivals and the Sabbath, since the destruction of the Temple raised some immediate questions. To Yohanan b. Zakkai is assigned a number of ordinances on how to observe the Festival of Sukkot and the New Year in the aftermath of the destruction of the Temple. These in context are represented as temporary matters, allowing for keeping the Festival in the interim before the Temple's reconstruction. The character of what the postwar authorities actually did, that is to say, an extensive corpus of legislation for the Temple and for rites closely associated with the Temple, will show us the unimportance of what is attributed to Yohanan b. Zakkai. For the critical issue was the Temple's place in the observance of the pilgrim festivals, and that issue would not be faced at this time. It had to be confronted only when it was clear that, for some time to come, Jerusalem would no longer be accessible. Then provision would be made for recording the way in which the pilgrim festivals had been observed, a way of affirming the hope that they would once more be kept. So the destruction of the Temple appears to have stimulated little effort to rethink the matter of the observance of Sabbath and festivals and brought about no creative impulse in this suggestive area of the ancient religion.

When fully worked out, the Mishnah's Division of Women would pay close attention to exchanges of property and documents attendant upon the transfer of a woman from her father's to her husband's house. Authorities between the wars provided only a little guidance for such matters. For a very long time before 70 the national, prevailing law must have defined and governed them. What is significant is that broader and nonsectarian matters, surely subject to a long history of accepted procedure, should have been raised at all. It means that, after the destruction, attention turned to matters which sectarians had not regarded as part of their realm of concern. This may have meant that others who had carried responsibility for the administration of public affairs, such as scribes, now made an appearance. And it also may have meant that the vision of the sectarians themselves had begun to broaden and to encompass the administration of the life of ordinary folk, not within the sect. Both meanings are to be imputed to the fact of interest in issues of public administration of property transfers along with the transfer of women to and from the father's home. Concern for definition of personal status devolves upon genealogical questions urgent to the priesthood, and, it follows, in the present stratum are contained matters of deep concern to yet a third constituency. But these matters of interest to scribes and priests do not predominate. It is their appearance, rather than their complete expression and articulation, which is of special interest.

If we ask what the Mishnah wishes to say in particular about the general themes which it has chosen for its Division of Women, it is difficult to specify a distinctive and telling message. Much appears to be so commonsensical that, with Scripture in hand, anyone might have reached the same conclusions. Take, for example, that stipulation in writs of divorce or in betrothals must be carried out or the acts are null; women must be supported if their marriages end because of divorce or death; conflicting claims of property must be adjudicated by the principle that the claimant must prove the validity of his or her claim; a wife loses her property rights if she violates the law of Moses. While, as I said above, the laws of Holy Things seem to me to yield paramount traits which express important ideas, those of Women do not. They are discrete. There is no underlying and unifying conception to be discerned in any major segment of the laws, still less in the law as a whole.

And yet if we cannot characterize as a whole the components of the system, we can claim that before us we do see the shape of the system as it would ultimately emerge. The one important element to come after the wars, attention to property exchanges attendant upon betrothal, surely is predictable at this point in the unfolding of the system. For a law which defines property transfers at the end of a marriage in due course must provide the same sorts of definitions for transfers which come at the beginning of a marriage. It follows that, by the end of the interim period, the system of Women was pretty well in hand. The tendency of the system, moreover, to overcome and transcend its sectarian origins and to begin to make rules applicable to the community at large, laws in their substance in now way productive of social divisiveness upon which the sect would depend for its continuing existence, is established.

New Perspectives

And that is the main point. The clearly implied aspiration of the laws was to apply to the Israelite world as a whole. That aspiration would not change. The context later on, moreover, would only confirm and intensify the original intention. For later on the authorities whose opinions find their way into the Mishnah would indeed take up a range of practical authority and recieve a kind of power which, before that time, they appear not to have had. It follows that a system aiming at governance of the Israelite world at large is brought to fulfillment and perfectly natural closure at that point at which the social and political aspirations which underlay the earliest, directly antecedent legislation were realized. Sages now aspired to imagine the authority which their successors would enjoy: the right to make those concrete and everyday decisions of the administration of trivialities which, all together, constitute the effective government of the Jewish people. What is remarkable, therefore, was the power of the imagination of the legislators of the day to contemplate a world they did not then know.

Whoever before 70 had settled those disputes about real estate, working conditions, debts and loans, torts and damages, and other sorts of conflicts which naturally came up in a vital and stable society, the group represented in the Mishnah did not. That is why the Division of Damages, dealing with civil law and government, contains virtually nothing assigned to authorities before the wars. Scribes in Temple times served as judges and courts within the Temple government, holding positions in such system of administration of the Israelite part of Palestine as the Romans left within Jewish control. The Division of Damages is remarkably reticent on what after the destruction they might have contributed out of the heritage of their earlier traditions and established practices. Materials of this period yield little evidence of access to any tradition prior to 70, except (predictably) for Scripture. When people at this time did take up topics relevant to the larger system of Damages, they directed their attention to the exegesis of Scriptures and produced results which clarify what Moses laid down, or which carry forward problems or topics suggested by the Torah. That is not evidence that thinkers of this period had access (or wished to gain access) to any source of information other than that one, long since available to the country as a whole, provided by Moses. It follows that, in so far as any materials at all relevant to the later Mishnaic system of Damages did come forth between the wars, the work appears to have begun from scratch. And not much work can have been done to begin with. There is no evidence of sustained and systematic thought about the topics assembled in the Division of Damages. We find some effort devoted to the exegesis of Scriptures relevant to the Division. But whether or not those particular passages were selected because of a large-scale inquiry into the requirements of civil law and government, or because of an overriding interest in a given set of Scriptures provoked by some other set of questions entirely, we cannot say.

The net result of the stage in the law's unfolding demarcated by the two wars is that history—the world-shattering events of the day—is kept at a distance from the center of life. The system of sustaining life shaped essentially within an ahistorical, indeed antihistorical, view of reality, goes forward in its own path, a way above history. Yet the facts of history are otherwise. The people as a whole can hardly be said to have accepted the ahistorical ontology framed by the sages and in part expressed by the systems of Purities, Agriculture, and Holy things. The people followed the path of Bar Kokhba and took the road to war once more. When the three generations had passed after the destruction and the historical occasion for restoration through historical—political and military—action came to fulfillment, the great war of 132 to 135 broke forth. A view of being in which people were seen to be moving toward some point within time, the fulfillment and the end of history as it was known, clearly shaped the consciousness of Israel after 70 just as had been the case in the decades before 70. So if to the sages of our system, history and the end of history were essentially beside the point and pivot, the construction of a world of cyclical eternities being the purpose and center, and the conduct of humble things like eating and drinking the paramount and decisive focus of the sacred, others saw things differently. To those who hoped and therefore fought, Israel's life had other meanings entirely.

The Second War proved still more calamitous than the First. In 70 the Temple was lost, in 135, even access to the city. In 70 the people, though suffering grievous losses, endured more or less intact. In 135 the land of Judah—surely the holiest part of the holy Land—evidently lost the bulk of its Jewish population. Temple, Land, people—all were gone in the forms in which they had been known. In the generation following the calamity of Bar Kokhba, what would be the effect upon the formation of the Mishnah? It is to that question that we now turn.

From Sectarian Fantasy to Social Vision:
After the Transition

Before the wars the people whose ideas come to full expression in the Mishnah formed a small group, perhaps to be categorized as a sect. If so, it was a cultic sect, a holiness order, expressing the aspirations of lay people to live as if they belonged to the caste of priests, and of priests to live as if the whole country were the Temple. It is no surprise that those definitive topics of the Mishnah which gain attention early on were the ones having to do with food and sex: how food is raised, the petty obsessions governing its preparation and consumption, and who may marry whom in the constrained circle of those who worried those small, compulsive worries. After the two wars, as we shall see in due course, the entire framework of the Mishnah would undergo revision. The range of topics so expanded that laws came to full expression to govern not merely the collective life of a small group but the political and social affairs of a whole nation. What had come from the then-distant past, from the preceding century, would be taken into caring hands and carefully nurtured, as if it mattered. But the fresh and the new challenge of an age of new beginnings would lead to daring choices: laws for real estate and commercial transactions, laws for the scribal profession and the documentation of changes in the status of people and property, laws, even, for the governance of the Temple, then in ruins, and the conduct of its rites throughout the cycle of appointed times and seasons, for the maintenance of the Temple and its caste of priests and Levites, and (of all things) for the design of the Temple when it woud be rebuilt and for the conduct of its everyday offering. All of this would follow in that remarkable time of fulfillment and closure which came in the aftermath of the wars.

What was achieved between them? Small things, little steps—a bridge between that completed statement constituted by the sectarian fantasy framed before the wars, and that also-completed statement about everything and everyone: the political vision, the social policy, the economic program, in full and glorious detail, which would be the closed and ample Mishnah itself. Describing Moslem philosophical visions of the world of the Greek philosophers, Peter Brown comments, "Only a civilization of impressive density can cause the previous culture of a millennium to spin into so strange an orbit'' (Brown, p. 31). When we consider the beginnings of it all in a narrowly priestly fantasy, acted out by a tight little circle of specialists in uncommon and egregious laws involving the contact of a loaf of bread of a specified status with a deceased reptile, we must wonder what swept the world out of the old and into the new orbit.

For, as I have just now stressed, the priestly vision, with its emphasis on the Temple as the pivot and the world as the periphery, the Temple as guarantor of life, the world as the threatening realm of death, the Temple as the security and strength of Israel, the world as its enemy, and, above all, the unreliable and perpetually threatening character of persons and substances on the borders between Temple and world— when we contemplate that vision, we must wonder that anyone could share it *and yet expand it.* That is just what happened. For the priestly component of the ultimate structure of the Mishnah remains paramount. Yet the Mishnah is not a priestly document. It is much more than that. As we know, had the Mishnah come to closure before the wars, it would have consisted of the system of uncleanness, fully exposed if lacking numerous details, a part of the system of agriculture, a system (quite its own) about food preparation, with emphasis upon doing so on special occasions (when the group presumably was able to come together), and, finally, a half-system on suitable marital candidates under special conditions, a set of laws calculated (if observed) to render members of the group unacceptable to non-members as marriage partners. Now, that version of the Mishnah spun about the Temple, in a stable orbit around the altar.

And the other Mishnah—the one we now have, pursues its predictable path in quite another orbit. It makes peripheral the Temple and its concerns, as they come to expression in everyday imitation of the priesthood. It treats as central other things entirely: civil and criminal law and political institutions and their power, in the Fourth Division; the conduct of the cult itself, not merely of people wishing to place themselves into relationship with a cult by setting their feet on a single continuous path to the altar, in the Second and Fifth Divisions; the web of documents which encase and protect transfers of persons and property, both in life and afterward, in the Third and Fourth Divisions; the full articulation of the rules governing the disposition of crops in accord with the holiness inhering in them, and the arrangement of relationships (hitherto remarkably ignored) between virtuosi of the law and outsiders so that all, all together, might constitute a single Israel, this in the First Division and in the Sixth. Now these changes, ultimately realized in the full expression and closure of the Mishnah itself, are no issue of small detail. They cut to the heart of the matter. They shift completely and ultimately the very center of focus of the document itself. They represent, as I said, a Mishnah wholly other than the Mishnah (if we may call it that) which would have taken shape before the wars, if anyone had thought to make one.

But, of course, so far as we know, no one did. So the truly stunning change effected after the wars was the formation of the book itself, the book which brought together the ideas and principles and laws in circulation before its time, and put them all together into something far more than the components, the paltry corpus of conceptions available to the framers of the document. Now we see with full clarity the ponderous movement from one orbit to the other, the shift of the previous culture of, if not a millennium, then at least nearly seven or eight hundred years (from the second century backward to the sixth). That old, reliable, priestly way of life and world view from the Temple mountain came to be subsumed by, and transformed into, a social vision, as I said, framed on the plane of Israel. What is stunning is the shift in perspective, not the change in what was to be seen. Merely seeing the Temple and its altar from a vantage point other than the Temple mount itself is a remarkable movement in perspective. Only framing a code of law framed in rules made of words in place of practice codified in gesture and studied act constitutes an astonishing shift in focus. From interests limited to the home and hearth the opening lens of social thought takes in a larger frame indeed: from home to court, from eating and drinking, beds and pots and pans, to exchanges of property and encounters of transactions in material power. What moved the world on its axis, the ball of earth in its majesty? The answer is self-evident: seventy years of wars and the tumult of wars. These shattered a hope which, to begin with, had little to do with the Temple at all. There was then a moment of utter despair about things which, from the perspective of the philosophers of the Mishnah, might as well have taken place on yet another planet (but, alas, things wholly within their experience). The previous culture of somewhat less than a millennium spun into another orbit, not because of the gravity of yet a new civilization of impressive density, though. The reason requires its own metaphor.

Part Two

THE SECOND CENTURY

Social Vision

4

THE SECOND CENTURY:
RECONSTRUCTION IN MIND

The Issues of the Age

The second-century Church Fathers refer to Christian heretics called
Gnostics, people who believed, among other things, that salvation
came from insightful knowledge of a god beyond the creator-god, and
of a fundamental flaw in creation revealed in the revealed Scriptures of
Moses. The Gnostic understands "who we were, and what we have
become; where we were . . . whither we are hastening; from what we
are being released; what birth is, and what is rebirth" (Pagels, p. xix).
This insight into the true condition of the believer derives not from
revelation but from self-knowledge, which is knowledge of God. Now
in introducing the viewpoint of second-century Gnostics and juxtapos-
ing their principal emphases with those of the Mishnah, I must empha-
size that we know no writings of Gnostics who were Jews. We cannot
claim that the viewpoint of Gnostic thinkers on two questions of
fundamental importance to the Mishnah—creation, revelation—derives from Israelites of the Land of Israel. The only certainty is that
the Mishnah takes up a position both specifically and totally at variance
with the position framed, on identical issues, by people writing in
exactly the same period. No one can claim that Gnostic and Mishnaic
thinkers addressed, or even knew about, one another. But they did
confront precisely the same issues, and when placed into juxtaposition
with one another, they present a striking and suggestive contrast. It is
that contrast which we now shall briefly contemplate.

If the apocalyptic prophets focused upon historical events and their
meaning, the Gnostic writers of the second century sought to escape
from the framework of history altogether. For Israel, Jerusalem had
become a forbidden city. The Temple had long stood as the pinnacle

47

of creation and now was destroyed. The Gnostic thinkers deemed creation, celebrated in the cult, to be a cosmic error. The destruction of the Temple had evoked the prophetic explanations of the earlier destruction and turned attention in the search for meaning in the destruction to the revealed Torah of God to Moses at Mount Sinai. The Gnostic thinkers declared the Torah to be a deceit, handed down by an evil creator. It is as if the cosmic issues vital to the first-century apocalyptic prophets were taken up one by one and declared closed, and closed in a negative decision, by the second-century Gnostics.

The Mishnah's Reaffirmation: Creation and Revelation

The thinkers of the Mishnah for their part addressed two principal issues also important to Gnostic thought, the worth of creation and the value of the Torah. They took a quite opposite position on both matters. The Mishnah's profoundly priestly celebration of creation and its slavishly literal repetition of what clearly is said in Scripture gain significance specifically in that very context in which, to others, these are subjected to a different, deeply negative, valuation. True, we have no evidence that Gnostics were in the Land of Israel and formed part of the people of Israel in the period in which the Mishnah reaches full expression and final closure. So we speak of a synchronic debate at best. In fact what we know in Gnostic writings is a frame of mind and a style of thought characteristic of others than Israelites, living in lands other than the Land of Israel. What justifies our invoking two ubiquitous and fundamental facts about Gnostic doctrine in the description of the context in which the Mishnah took shape is the simple fact that, at the critical points in its structure, the Mishnaic system counters what are in fact two fundamental and generative assertions of all Gnostic systems. Whether or not there were Gnostics known to Mishnah's philosophers, who, specifically in response to the destruction and permanent prohibition of the Temple, declared to be lies and deceit the creation celebrated in the Temple and the Torah governing there, we do not know. But these would be appropriate conclusions to draw from the undisputed facts of the hour in any case. The Temple designed by the Torah for celebrating the center and heart of creation was no more. Would this not have meant that the creator of the known creation and revealer of the Torah, the allegedly one God behind both, is either weak or evil? And should the elect not aspire to escape from the realm of creation and the power of the demiurge? And who will pay heed to what is written in the revelation of creation, Temple, and Torah? These seem to me conclusions distinctively suitable to be drawn from the ultimate end of the thousand-year-old cult: the final and total discrediting of the long-pursued, eternally fraudulent hope for messianic deliverance in this time, in this world, and in this life. So it would have been deemed wise for those who know to seek and celebrate a different salvation, coming from a god unknown in this world, unrevealed in this world's revelation, not responsible for the infelicitous condition of creation.

Second-Century Gnosticism

For our purposes, therefore, when we speak of Gnosticism as relevant, we refer, in Wilson's happy phrase to "an atmosphere, not a system" (Wilson, p. 261). In so far as Gnosticism incorporated a cosmic solution to the problem of evil, the Gnostic mode of thought had the power to confront the disaster of Israel's two wars against Rome and their metaphysical consequences. The Gnostic solution, if we may posit what someone might have been intelligent to conclude, is not difficult to discern. These events proved beyond doubt the flaw in creation, for the Temple had been the archetype of creation. The catastrophes demonstrated the evil character of the creator of this world. The catastrophes required the conclusion that there is another mode of being, another world beyond this one of creation and cult. So, whatever positive doctrines may or may not have found adherents among disappointed Israelites of the later first and second centuries, there are these two negative conclusions which anyone moving out of the framework of the cult, priesthood, and Temple, with its Torah, celebration of creation and the creator, and affirmation of this world and its creations, would have had to reach. First, the creator is not good. Second, the Torah, the record of creator and the will of the creator, is false.

Later Gnostic cosmogonies take as their primary problem the explanation not of the creation of the world but of the origin of man and of evil (Wilson, p. 172). A flaw in creation accounts for the condition of the world, and this led to the conviction that the creator-god was evil. Wilson states, "The Gnostic, convinced of the evil of matter and regarding this world as under the sway of powers hostile to man, considered the Creator as one of these powers and so introduced a distinction between him and the supreme God" (Wilson, p. 184). The creator is a hostile being, the supreme god is not. The evil of human existence forces a dualism of a radical character (Wilson, p. 188). The created world is only the lowest stage of being; there are numbers of heavens above. Man really belongs not to this world but to a higher, heavenly world (Wilson, p. 207): "The essential feature in the Gnostic view of man is that he is really a divine being imprisoned in this

material world and separated by the barrier of the seven heavens from
his true abode. Salvation from fate, from body, from the bondage of
matter, from the changes and chances of this life, all the ills to which
the flesh is heir, is attained by gnosis, which may mean anything from
knowledge imparted in a mystic initiation to a purely magical knowledge of names and spells" (Wilson, p. 215).

Withdrawal to inwardness or despair of the world is a principal trait
of the Gnosticism of Nag Hammadi's library too. That accounts for
the Jewish contribution to Gnosticism: to designate the God of the
Hebrew Scriptures as "the malevolent force whose misguided blunder
produced the world, a God who was ignorant of the hidden good God
beyond" (*Nag Hammadi*, p. 6). The Testimony of Truth states matters
very simply: "For no one who is under the Law will be able to look up
to the truth, for they will not be able to serve two masters. For the
defilement of the Law is manifest; but undefilement belongs to the
light" (*Nag Hammadi*, p. 18). When the Mishnah repeatedly resorts
to Scripture's facts to restate Scripture's opinion on virtually every
important topic of the Mosaic law codes (see chapter 5, below), this
judgment of the character of the law becomes a powerful and affirmative statement of the rejected alternative. Knowing what the framers
of the Mishnah chose not to say and do, which is what others did do,
we begin to make sense of what the framers of Mishnah did have to
say and did choose to do.

In as much as the Mishnah reaches its systematic fullness after the
Second War against Rome, therefore, its framers have no choice but
to address and compose a response to the inescapable issues of the
day. These are defined by the facts that, first, Israelites no longer
could even enter Jerusalem; and, second, the Third Temple clearly
would not be restored in accord with the historical and mythic pattern
of the Scriptural account of the destruction of the First and the building
of the Second. That is to say, three generations had passed from 70 to
the war led by Bar Kokhba. But instead of a restoration came war.
And the road to war, through suffering and courage, in the end did not
lead Israel back to Zion's mountain. People who wished to read
Scripture as a set of accounts of how things should happen now could
find little grounds for hope. Indeed, confidence in the veracity of the
Mosaic revelation and in the goodness of God who had revealed the
Torah to Moses can only have been severely shaken, as Ezra and
Baruch have shown us. For fair numbers of people, it appears to have
fallen to ruins. In the rubble of once-high hopes were buried the legacy
of centuries of prophetic apocalypse. Misshapen stones formed themselves into patterns of despair,, detritus signifying nothing but itself,
ruins of hope, ruins of history.

Choices Made by Others

As I said, we simply do not know that there even were Gnostics in the Land of Israel, let alone within the Israelite community known to the sages of the Mishnah. All we know is that, in the same time as the Mishnah's formation and promulgation, Christian communities from France to Egypt encompassed groups which took a position sharply at variance with that of the Hebrew Scriptures affirmed in the Church in general on precisely the questions of creation and revelation and redemption confronting the Israelite world of the second century. Among the many and diverse positions taken up in the systems reported by Christian writers or now documented through Christian-Gnostic writings found at Nag Hammadi there are three which, as I have emphasized, are remarkably pertinent. First, the creator-god is evil, because, second, creation is deeply flawed. Third, revelation as Torah is a lie. These conclusions yield, for one Gnostic-Christian thinker after another, the simple proposition that redemption is gained in escape; this world is to be abandoned, not constructed, affirmed, and faithfully tended in painstaking detail. It is in the context of this widespread negative judgment on the very matters on which, for their part, the Mishnah's sages register a highly affirmative opinion, that the choices made by the framers of the Mishnah become fully accessible.

Characterizing the Mishnah's ultimate system as a whole, we may call it both locative and utopian, in that it focuses upon Temple but is serviceable anywhere. In comparison to the Gnostic systems, it is, similarly, profoundly Scriptural; but it also is deeply indifferent to Scripture, drawing heavily upon the information supplied by Scripture for the construction and expression of its own systemic construction, which in form and language is wholly independent of any earlier Israelite document (see chapter 5, below). It is, finally, a statement of affirmation of this world, of the realm of society, state, and commerce, and at the same time a vigorous denial that how things are is how things should be, or will be. For the Mishnaic system speaks of the building of a state, government, and civil and criminal system, of the conduct of transactions of property, commercce, trade, of forming the economic unit of a family through transfer of women and property and the ending of such a family-economic unit, and similar matters, touching all manner of dull details of ordinary and everyday life (see chapter 4, below).

So the Mishnah's framers deemed the conduct of ordinary life in this world to be the critical focus and central point of tension of all being. At the same time, their account of these matters drew more heavily upon Scripture than upon any more contemporary and practical source. The philosophers designed a government and a state utterly out of phase with the political realities of the day, speaking, as we shall see, of king and high priest, but never of sage, patriarch, and Roman official. They addressed a lost world of Temple cult as described by the Torah, of cleanness, support of priesthood, offerings on ordinary days and on appointed times in accord with Torah law, and so mapped out vast tracts of a territory whose only reality lay in people's imagination, shaped by Scripture. Mishnah's map is not territory.

Accordingly, for all its intense practicality and methodical application of the power of practical reason and logic to concrete and material things, the Mishnah presents a made-up system which, in its way, is no more practical or applicable in all ways to ordinary life than are the diverse systems of philosophy and myth, produced in its day in other parts of the world, which fall under the name, Gnostic.

What the framers of the Mishnah have in common with the framers of the diverse world constructions of the Gnostic sort thus is, first, a system building, and, second, confrontation with two issues addressed in the diverse Gnostic systems of antiquity, the nature of creation and the creator and the character of the revelation of the creator-god. If in conclusion I may state in a few simple words the position of the Mishnah on these two burning issues of the day, it is that creation is good and worthy of man's best consideration, and that the creator of the world is good and worthy of man's deepest devotion. So out of ccreation and revelation will come redemption. The Torah is not only not false but the principal source of truth. A system which intersects with the rules of the Torah therefore will patiently and carefully restate, and, so, blatantly reaffirm, precisely what Scripture has to say about those same points in common. A structure coming in the aftermath of the Temple's destruction which doggedly restated rules governing the Temple so reaffirmed, in the most obvious possible way, the cult and the created world celebrated therein. For as soon as we speak of sacrifice and Temple, as 2 Baruch has shown us, we address the questions of creation and the value of the created world and of redemption. When, therefore, a document emerges rich in discourse on these matters and doggedly repetitive of precisely what Scripture says about exactly the same things, the meaning in context is clear.

5

THE MISHNAH AS A SYSTEM OF JUDAISM

The Aftermath of War

While the Mishnah contains opinions and laws reflecting the age before 70, and also the one from 70 to 135, whatever came down from those periods was completely reworked afterward, between 135 and 200. The document, when complete, moreover, contained a vast amount of new material. We may regard the whole system of the Mishnah as the work of the second century. Indeed, there is much reason to regard the bulk of the work of building the system as complete within the single generation after the Bar Kokhba War, from about 135 to about 160. Our present task, therefore, is to turn to a description of the Mishnah as a whole and complete statement.

To do so we turn to a description of the six divisions which constitute the system, and, further, to the tractates which make up these divisions. Each tractate, within a division, takes up a problem or a theme or a single topic, e.g., Temple sacrifices, the structure of government (Sanhedrin), or writs of divorce. As I shall explain, knowing what topic informs a tractate does not allow us to predict what the framers of that tractate will want to know *about* that topic. The Mishnah wishes to do anything but supply mere facts. It raises and solves problems. Each topic has an importance to the system of the Mishnah as a whole. While a fair number of tractates is at best informative, the larger number makes the effort to ask an insistent question about a tractate's topic. It is in pressing that question that the shape and structure of the ideas about the topic are worked out and fully exposed.

Seeing the Whole

We now turn to examine the Mishnah's tractates as such, seeing them, from the pinnacle of the complete Divisions of which they form component parts. In order to do this, what we want to know is the way in which the stated topic of a tractate is unpacked and spread out. What people wish to say about a given topic and how their ideas are ordered are the two critical points of interest in this part of the descriptive work. Knowing how they define the issues of a theme, what they wish to know about a given topic, as we take into account all the other things about which they do not ask, will lead us to the wide perspective of the Mishnah as a complete and intelligible statement. Once we have that statement clearly in mind, the framers of the Mishnah and its philosophers made their comment.

In turning from isolated details of the law to an account of the generative problematic of the several tractates, we rely upon a simple device. If we want to know what people thought important about a topic, we have to begin by examining the way in which they simply organize their ideas on that topic. This means two things. First, what aspects of the topic do they treat? Second, in what order do they treat them? A clear picture of how ideas are laid out tells us what people wish to know about a given topic, it is a small step to ask what they think important. So sequence yields a picture of order. The fact of an orderly arrangement of ideas is the principal exegetical device in our hands. Since it is feasible to outline every tractate and to present a clearly orderly account of each topic, the work is entirely suitable to the evidence, and the evidence—the Mishnah—is appropriate to the question raised about it. That is to say, what we shall see time and again is that the framers' mode of organization reveals very clearly, right on the surface, the blatant outline of precisely what the framers of that tractate deemed critical about the topic under discussion.

What is required is a simple statement of a topic and what the philosophers of the Mishnah tractate devoted to said topic thought important to say about it. This statement is given in the present chapter. In this way the topical unfolding of the Mishnah, Division by Division, as a whole, will be fully and totally laid out before the reader. It is a tribute to the genius at form and order of the ultimate framers of the Mishnah that such a procedure is possible. It is a tribute to the genius at philosophy of the thinkers of the Mishnah that such a procedure actually can be, and I think is, interesting and compelling.

The Division of Agriculture

The Division of Agriculture as it has come down to us treats two topics, first, producing crops in accord with the Scriptural rules on the subject, second, paying the required offerings and tithes to the priests, Levites, and poor. The principal point of the Division is that the Land is holy, because God has a claim both on it and upon what it produces. God's claim must be honored by setting aside a portion of the produce for those for whom God has designated it. God's ownership must be acknowledged by observing the rules God has laid down for use of the Land. In sum, the Division is divided along these lines: (1) Rules for producing crops in a state of holiness—tractates Kilayim, Shebiit, Orlah; (2) Rules for disposing of crops in accord with the rules of holiness—tractates Peah, Demai, Terumot, Maaserot, Maaser Sheni, Hallah, Bikkurim, Berakhot.

The theory of the Division of Agriculture on the tithing laws is expressed by Richard S. Sarason. Since Sarason here has done the preliminary work of systematic description for this part of the Division, I shall quote his account at length.

Mishnah's primary concern [in this portion of the Division of Agriculture] is with the process of sanctification of the various agricultural offerings, and, particularly, in the part which man plays in the process of sanctification. In this respect, I think it hardly coincidental that the lengthiest tractate in the Order of Seeds is Terumot, which deals with that offering regarded by Mishnah as holy *par excellence*. Nor is it coincidental that Mishnah devotes a tractate to second tithe, which is deemed holy, but not to the Levitical first tithe, which is not sanctified. The tractates on tithing give us a kind of geometry or logic of the sacred and sanctification in the realm of agricultural produce. A careful analysis of these tractates will show that Mishnah's theory of the holiness of produce which grows from the soil of the Land of Israel is transactional. That is to say, holiness does not naturally inhere in produce. Rather, God and man are the agents of sanctification. God, as owner of the Land, has a prior claim on its produce. But man must acknowledge God's ownership, and validate God's claim through actively designating and separating God's portion. Additionally, holiness is to be understood primarily in functional rather than substantive terms, i.e., that which is deemed holy belongs to God (and frequently is allotted by God to his priests), and must not be used by ordinary Israelites. Sacrilege thus is conceived as a violation of God's property rights.

The authorities behind Mishnah primarily are interested in spelling out the role of human action and, particularly, intention in the process of sanctification. That role is determinative throughout the process. To begin with, the locus of susceptibility to sanctification is determined with reference to man's actions and intentions (cf. Tractate Maaserot). Not everything that grows in the soil of the Land of Israel is liable to the separation of heave-offering and tithes. Liability falls only on produce which is cultivated for human food (M. Ma. 1:1). This notion, of course, begins in Scripture, which requires Israelite farmers to offer to God, as owner of the Land, the best part of their grain, wine, and oil, and to feed the priests and

Levites, who do not farm the land. Mishnah expands the liability to include all edible produce. The tithing laws, then, are food laws. Only produce which can be human food enters the system of tithing and sanctification.

Similarly, the point at which produce becomes liable to the separation of *terumah* and tithes (i.e., becomes *tebel;* see below) is the point at which it becomes edible (M. Ma. 1:2). But man's actions and intentions further determine liability at this juncture. For before edible produce has been fully harvested or processed, it may be eaten randomly without inucrring liability to tithing. Only if a man eats the produce as a regular meal before it is harvested must he tithe it. Furthermore, the point at which produce is considered to be fully harvested and liable to tithing also is determined by human intention regarding its ultimate disposition. If the farmer intends to bring his produce to market, it becomes liable to tithing when it is in that condition in which it will be brought to market—sifted, stacked, tied in bundles. If, on the other hand, he intends to bring the produce home to be eaten by his household, it does not become liable to tithing until it enters his private domain—the house or the courtyard.

Finally, produce becomes holy (i.e., God's property) only through man's act of consecration. This is made clear by considering the status of *tebel,* i.e. produce which has become liable to the separation of *terumah* and tithes, but from which these offerings have not yet been separated. Such produce must not be eaten by man, nor may benefit be derived from its use. But this is not because the produce now is deemed "holy," rather because it is now susceptible to sanctification, where previously it had not been. The whole is deemed "bonded" to God until his portion has been designated by the farmer's verbal declaration, and then separated. Even the priest, the ultimate recipient of the most holy portions (*terumah, terumat ma'aśer*) has no share in them until they actually have been separated. Before that time, these offerings exist only *in potentia.* For the same reason, *tebel* is treated as unconsecrated produce, rather than as *terumah,* regarding removes of uncleanness—the *terumah* does not come into being until it has been designated.

To summarize: Mishnah's theory of holiness in *Seder Zera'im* is transactional rather than immanentist. Nothing (except perhaps for God) is inherently sacred. The Land of Israel is sanctified through its relationship to God. The produce of the Lord is sanctified by man, acting under God's commandment, through verbal designation and separation of the various offerings. Man, through his action and intention, additionally determines what is susceptible to sanctification (i.e., liable to tithing as human food), and the point at which it is susceptible (i.e., edible, at the point of completion of processing or harvesting, or the point of intention to make a fixed meal). Mishnah's primary concern in the tractates under investigation is that man should separate properly that which is due to God, so that non-priests will not inadvertently eat produce bonded to God or consecrated to him. Mishnah's authorities further wish to examine in detail man's role in the process of sanctification, and to specify the power of his will, word, and deed. ["Mishnah"]

This account of the main issues of the Division of Agriculture correlates with what we shall see when we turn to the succeeding Divisions.

The Division of Appointed Times

The Mishnaic Division of Appointed Times forms a system in which the advent of a holy day, like the Sabbath of creation, sanctifies the life of the Israelite village through imposing on the village rules on the model of those of the Temple. The purpose of the system, therefore, is to bring into alignment the moment of sanctification of the village and the life of the home with the moment of sanctification of the Temple on those same occasions of appointed times. The underlying and generative theory of the system is that the village is the mirror image of the Temple. If things are done in one way in the Temple, they will be done in the opposite way in the village. Together the village and the Temple on the occasion of the holy day therefore form a single continuum, a completed creation, thus awaiting sanctification.

The village is made like the Temple in that on appointed times one may not freely cross the lines distinguishing the village from the rest of the world, just as one may not freely cross the lines distinguishing the Temple from the world. But the village is a mirror image of the Temple. The boundary lines prevent free entry into the Temple, so they restrict free egress from the village. On the holy day what one may do in the Temple is precisely what one may *not* do in the village. So the advent of the holy day affects the village by bringing it into sacred symmetry in such wise as to effect a system of opposites; each is holy, in a way precisely the opposite of the other. Because of the underlying conception of perfection attained through the union of opposites, the village is not represented as conforming to the model of the cult, but of constituting its antithesis.

The world thus regains perfection when on the holy day heaven and earth are united, the whole completed and done: the heaven, the earth, and all their hosts. This moment of perfection renders the events of ordinary time, of "history," essentially irrelevant. For what really matters in time is that moment in which sacred time intervenes and effects the perfection formed of the union of heaven and earth, of Temple, in the model of the former, and Israel, its complement. It is not a return to a perfect time but a recovery of perfect being, a fulfillment of creation, which explains the essentially ahistorical character of the Mishnah's Division on Appointed Times. Sanctification constitutes an ontological category and is effected by the creator.

This explains why the Division in its rich detail is composed of two quite distinct sets of materials. First, it addresses what one does in the sacred space of the Temple on the occasion of sacred time, as distinct from what one does in that same sacred space on ordinary, undifferentiated days, which is a subject worked out in Holy Things. Second, the Division defines how for the occasion of the holy day one creates a corresponding space in one's own circumstance, and what one does, within that space, during sacred time. The issue of the Temple and cult on the special occasion of festivals is treated in tractates Pesahim, Sheqalim, Yoma, Sukkah, and Hagigah. Three further tractates, Rosh Hashanah, Taanit, and Megillah, are necessary to complete the discussion. The matter of the rigid definition of the outlines in the village, of a sacred space, delineated by the limits within which one may move on the Sabbath and festival, and of the specification of those things which one may and may not do within that space in sacred time, is specified in Shabbat, Erubin, Besah, and Moed Qatan.

While the twelve tractates of the Division appear to fall into two distinct groups, joined merely by a common theme, in fact they relate through a shared, generative metaphor. It is, as I said, the comparison, in the context of sacred time, of the spatial life of the Temple to the spatial life of the village, with activities and restrictions to be specified for each, upon the common occasion of the Sabbath or festival. The Mishnah's purpose therefore is to correlate the sanctity of the Temple, as defined by the holy day, with the restrictions of space and of action which make the life of the village different and holy, as defined by the holy day.

The Mishnah clearly has its notion of what is important about an occasion, "great day," "day of the Lord," or "holy day." In so far as it wishes to take up the meaning of "time," in the concrete framework in which the Mishnah carries on its discussion of any topic, it is in the present Division that the Mishnah makes its judgments. There are other ways in which philosophers of the same period as the Mishnah—the first and second centuries—formulate and work out the same general range of issues as are before us. To grasp the full weight and meaning of what the Mishnah chooses for its program of thought, we have to allude to the things the framers of the Mishnah, like others of their age, might have done, but clearly do not wish to do.

This is a very specific matter. The Mishnah does *not* propose an abstract essay on the nature of time, the meaning of history. It also does not draw the contrast between this age and the world to come, as we saw in Baruch and Ezra. This Division's framers do not reflect on any number of other mythic or philosophical conceptions which may be taken up and used to fill out with concrete substance the abstract conception of time. Indeed, when we consider the range of topics and themes—historical and messianic—available for inclusion in a Division devoted to the passage of seasons and sanctification of time, the festivals and, by extension, the meaning of this perpetual change and movement against the background of history, we must be astonished at the highly restricted agendum, cultic and ahistorical, laid forth by the Mishnah. The very conception of appointed time is allowed only one meaning. Unlike the recurrent emphasis of Deuteronomy, the Sabbath or festival is no longer a theme or topic available for referring to some moment in historical time, to something which happened to Israel. The theme does not speak of an occasion chosen and set forth long ago and now nearing realization—"next year at this time." Since "appointed time" may be used for diverse, one-time and deeply historical occasions, it is important to recognize what the Mishnah finds suitable or unsuitable as a reference. The Mishnah refers in Appointed Times solely to recurrent events, embedded in the regular lunar calendar, defined, in nature, by the movement of the seasons and the moon, and, in Scripture, in the main by the affairs of the cult. The festivals are important in the cult and its counterpart. What recurs is the perfection of creation through the reunion of opposites. That is what is expressed in the Mishnah's problems and laws.

When the Mishnah speaks of appointed times, it means not the end-time or the one-time fulfillment of time but recurrent Sabbaths and festivals, new moons and holy days. When the Mishnah asks what is to be done in response to those appointed times of nature and cult, it answers in terms of cooking and eating, working and resting, sleeping, celebrating, and rejoicing. The Mishnah's program for Sabbaths and festivals speaks not of a being other than the ordinary life of Israel, but of a heightened enjoyment of everyday pleasures. The reason is not a rejection of cosmic myth, such as Smith described (see above, pp. 7–8), but the compelling presence of a different myth of being. The Mishnah does not contemplate some age other than the present one. When it speaks of time, it does not mean history at all. (Indeed, in the Division of Damages the Mishnah finds it possible to design a complete political system without once referring to historical reality or making provision at any point whatsoever for time and for change.) The framers of the document, moreover, so lay out matters that the sole provision in the village is for comfort and relaxation. If there is interest in that realm of power and force in which the mythological cosmic drama is played out, that heightened reality of mythic being realized in the holy time of Sabbaths and festivals is not permitted to come to expression at all in the Mishnah's restrictive terms. The reason for the Mishnah's worldliness is its otherworldly conception of the this-worldly life of Israel. What corresponds to heaven and complements heaven is heaven's projection onto earth, the Israelites in their villages. Here we have a different cosmic myth, which speaks of different things to different people.

The Division of Women

The Mishnaic system of Women defines the position of women in the social economy of Israel's supernatural and natural reality. That position acquires definition wholly in relationship to men, who impart form to the Israelite social economy. It is effected through both supernatural and natural, this-worldly action. What man and woman do on earth provokes a response in heaven, and the correspondences are perfect. So the position of women is defined and secured both in heaven and on earth. A correctly prepared writ of divorce on earth changes the status of the woman to whom it is given, so that in heaven she is available for sanctification to some other man, while, without that same writ, in heaven's view, should she go to some other man, she would be liable to be put to death. The earthly deed and the heavenly perspective correlate. That is indeed very much part of a larger system, which says the same thing over and over again.

The formation of the marriage comes under discussion in Qiddushin and Ketubot, as well as in Yebamot. The rules for the duration of the marriage are scattered throughout, but derive especially from parts of Ketubot, Nedarim, and Nazir, on the one side, and the paramount unit of Sotah, on the other. The dissolution of the marriage is dealt with in Gittin, as well as in Yebamot. We see very clearly, therefore, that important overall are issues of the transfer of property, along with women, covered in Ketubot and to some measure in Qiddushin, and the proper documentation of the transfer of women and property, treated in Ketubot and Gittin. The critical issues therefore turn upon legal documents—writs of divorce, for example—and legal recognition of changes in the ownership of property, e.g., through the collection of the settlement of a marriage contract by a widow, through the provision of a dowry, or through the disposition of the property of a woman during the period in which she is married. Within this orderly world of documentary and procedural concerns a place is made for the disorderly conception of the marriage not formed by human volition but decreed in heaven, the levirate connection. Yebamot states that super-nature sanctifies a woman to a man (under the conditions of the levirate connection). What it says by indirection is that man sanctifies too: man, like God, can sanctify that relationship between a man and a woman, and can also effect the cessation of the sanctity of that same relationship.

To the message and the purpose of the system of Women, woman is essential and central. But she is not critical. She sets the stage for the processes of the sacred. It is she who can be made sacred to man. It is she who ceases to stand within a man's sacred circle. But God and man, the latter through the documentary expression of his will and intention, possess the active power of sanctification. Like the holy Land of Agriculture, the holy Temple of Holy Things, and the potentially holy realm of the clean of Purities, women for the Division of Women define a principal part of the Mishnah's orderly conception of reality. Women form a chief component of the six-part realm of the sacred. It is, as I said, their position in the social economy of the Israelite reality, natural and supernatural, which is the subject of the Division and its tractates. But the whole—the six-part realm—is always important in *relationship* to man on earth and God in Heaven. Man and God effect the transaction. Sanctification is effected through process and through relationship. The center of logical tension is at critical relationships. The problematic of the subject is generated at the critical points of the relationship. The relationship—that is, the process or transaction—is what makes holy or marks as profane. God and man shape that process. Food grown from the earth, woman, cult, and the cultlike realm of the clean—these foci of the sacred form that inert matter made holy or marked as profane by the will and deed of God and of man, who is like God.

From the Mishnah's perspective, women are abnormal; men are normal. The reason the framers of the Mishnah choose to work out a Division on women flows from that fact. Women are something out of the ordinary. That is why they form a focus of sanctification: restoration of the extraordinary to the ordinary and the normal. The Mishnah cannot declare a dead creeping thing clean. The Mishnah cannot make women into men. It can provide for the purification of what is made unclean. It can provide for a world in which it is normal for woman to be subject to man, father or husband, and a system which regularizes the transfer of women from the hand of the father to that of the husband. The regulation of the transfer of women is the Mishnah's way of effecting the sanctification of what, for the moment, disturbs and disorders the orderly world. The work of sanctification becomes necessary in particular at the point of danger and disorder. An order of women must be devoted, therefore, to just these things, so as to preserve the normal modes of creation (''how these things really are''). Maleness, that is, normality, thus may encompass all, even and especially at the critical point of transfer.

In this connection the process outlined, as we shall see, in the

Division of Purities for the restoration of normality, meaning of cleanness, to what is abnormal, meaning uncleanness, is suggestive. What the Mishnah proposes is to restore the equilibrium disturbed by the encounter with the disruptive, disorganizing, and abnormal sources of uncleanness specified in the priestly writings. So the Division of Purities centers attention on the point of abnormality and its restoration to normality: sources of uncleanness, foci of uncleanness, modes of purification. Now, when we reflect on the view of women contained in the Mishnah, we observe a parallel interest in the point of abnormality and the restoration to normality of women: the moment at which a woman changes hands.

About woman as wife the Mishnah has little to say; about woman as mother, I cannot think of ten relevant lines in the Mishnah's Division of Woman. For these are not the topics to which the Mishnah will devote itself. The three systemically anomalous tractates from this perspective are not so far out of line. Sotah, of course, attends to the wife who is not a good wife. Nedarim, bearing Nazir in its wake, treats those moments specified by Scripture as especially important in the daughter's relationship to the father or the wife's to the husband. These are moments at which the father or the husband may intervene in the relationship of daughter or wife to God. In the present context, the relationship is unruly and dangerous, exactly like the relationship of daughter leaving father or of wife leaving husband, that is, at the critical moment of betrothal and consummation of the marriage, with attendant property settlement; or divorce or husband's death, at the critical moment of the dissolution of the marriage, with attendant property settlement.

An anomaly for the Mishnah is a situation requiring human intervention so that affairs may be brought into stasis, that is, made to conform with the heavenly projections of the created world. That quest for stasis, order, and regulation, which constitute wholeness and completeness, in the Division of Women leads the Mishnah to take up yet another circumstance of uncertainty. This it confronts at its most uncertain; just as the Division of Agriculture treats crops neither holy nor secular, so the system subjects the anomaly of woman to the capacity for ordering and regulating which is the gift and skill of priests and scribes.

The anomaly of woman therefore is addressed at its most anomalous. Yet the very essence of the anomaly, woman's sexuality, is scarcely mentioned. But it always is just beneath the surface. For what defines the woman's status—what is rarely made explicit in the Division of Women—is not whether or not she may have sexual relations, but with whom she may have them and with what consequence. It is assumed that, from long before the advent of puberty, a girl may be married and in any event is a candidate for sexuality. From puberty onward she will be married. But what is selected for intense and continuing concern is with whom she may legitimately marry, and with what economic and social effect. There is no sexual deed without public consequence; and only rarely will a sexual deed not yield economic results, in the transfer of property from one hand to another. So, as I said, what is anomalous is the woman's sexuality, which is treated in a way wholly different from man's. And the goal and purpose of the Mishnah's Division of Women are to bring under control and force into stasis all of the wild and unruly potentialities of sexuality, with their dreadful threat of uncontrolled shifts in personal status and material possession alike.

The Mishnah thus invokes heaven's interest in the most critical moment—whether Appointed Times or harvest time or hymeneal season—for individual and society alike. Its conception is that what is rightly done on earth is confirmed in heaven. A married woman who has sexual relations with any man but her husband has not merely committed a crime on earth. She has sinned against heaven. It follows that when a married woman receives a writ of divorce and so is free to enter into relationships with any man of her choosing, heaven's perceptions of that woman are affected just as much as are those of man on earth. What was beforehand a crime and a sin afterward is holy. The woman may contract a new marriage on earth which heaven, for its part, will oversee and sanctify. What is stated in these simple propositions is that those crucial and critical turnings at which a woman changes hands produce concern and response in heaven above as much as on earth below. And the reason, as I suggested at the beginning, is that heaven is invoked specifically at those times, and in those circumstances, in which Mishnah confronts a situation of anomaly, changes or disorder and proposes to effect suitable regulation and besought order.

The Division of Damages after the Wars

The Division of Damages comprises two subsystems, which fit together in a logical way. One part presents rules for the normal conduct of civil society. These cover commerce, trade, real estate, and other matters of everyday intercourse, as well as mishaps, such as damages by chattels and persons, fraud, overcharge, interest, and the like, in that same context of everyday social life. The other part describes the institutions governing the normal conduct of civil society, that is, courts of administration, and the penalties at the disposal of the government for the enforcement of the law. The two subjects form a single tight and systematic dissertation on the nature of Israelite society and its economic, social, and political relationships, as the Mishnah envisages them.

The main point of the first of the two parts of the Division is expressed in the sustained unfolding of the three Babas, Baba Qamma, Baba Mesia, and Baba Batra. It is that the task of society is to maintain perfect stasis, to preserve the prevailing situation, and to secure the stability of all relationships. To this end, in the interchanges of buying and selling, giving and taking, borrowing and lending, it is important that there be an essential equality of exchange. No party in the end should have more than what he had at the outset, and none should be the victim of a sizable shift in fortune and circumstance. All parties' rights to, and in, this stable and unchanging economy of society are to be preserved. When the condition of a person is violated, so far as possible the law will secure the restoration of the antecedent status.

An appropriate appendix to the Babas is at Abodah Zarah, which deals with the orderly governance of transactions and relationships between Israelite society and the outside world, the realm of idolatry, relationships which are subject to certain special considerations. These are generated by the fact that Israelites may not derive benefit (e.g., through commercial transactions) from anything which has served in the worship of an idol. Consequently, commercial transactions suffer limitations on account of extrinsic considerations of cultic taboos. While these cover both special occasions, e.g., fairs and festivals of idolatry, and general matters, that is, what Israelites may buy and sell, the main practical illustrations of the principles of the matter pertain to wine. The Mishnah supposes that gentiles routinely make use, for a libation, of a drop of any sort of wine to which they have access. It therefore is taken for granted that wine over which gentiles have had control is forbidden for Israelite use, and also that such wine is prohibited for Israelites to buy and sell. This other matter—ordinary everyday relationships with the gentile world, with special reference to trade and commerce—concludes what the Mishnah has to say about all those matters of civil and criminal law which together define everyday relationships within the Israelite nation and between that nation and all others in the world among whom, in Palestine as abroad, they lived side by side.

The other part of the Division describes the institutions of Israelite government and politics. This is in two main aspects, first, the description of the institutions and their jurisdiction, with reference to courts, conceived as both judicial and administrative agencies, and, second, the extensive discussion of criminal penalties. The penalties are three: death, banishment, and flogging. There are four ways by which a person convicted of a capital crime may be put to death. The Mishnah organizes a vast amount of information on what sorts of capital crimes are punishable by which of the four modes of execution. That information is alleged to derive from Scripture. But the facts are many, and the relevant verses few. What the Mishnah clearly contributes to this exercise is a first-rate piece of organization and elucidation of available facts. Where the facts come from we do not know. The Mishnah tractate Sanhedrin further describes the way in which trials are conducted in both monetary and capital cases and pays attention to the possibilities of perjury. The matter of banishment brings the Mishnah to a rather routine restatement of punishment by flogging and the application of that mode of punishment concludes the discussion.

These matters, worked out at Sanhedrin-Makkot, are supplemented in two tractates, Shebuot and Horayot, both emerging from Scripture. Lev. 5 and 6 refer to various oaths which apply mainly, though not exclusively, in courts. Lev. 4 deals with errors of judgment inadvertently made and carried out by the high priest, the ruler, and the people; the Mishnah knows that these considerations apply to Israelite courts too. What for Leviticus draws the chapters together is their common interest in the guilt offering, which is owing for violation of the rather diverse matters under discussion. Now in tractates Shebuot and Horayot the materials of Lev. 5–6 and 4, respectively, are worked out. But here it is from the viewpoint of the oath or erroneous instruction, rather than the cultic penalty. In Shebuot the discussion is intellectually imaginative and thorough, in Horayot, routine. The relevance of both to the issues of Sanhedrin and Makkot is obvious. For the matter of oaths in the main enriches the discussion of the conduct of the courts. The possibility of error is principally in the courts and other political institutions. So the four tractates on institutions and their functioning form a remarkably unified and cogent set.

The goal of the system of civil law is the recovery of the prevailing order and balance, the preservation of the established wholeness of the social economy. This idea is powerfully expressed in the organization of the three Babas, which treat first abnormal and then normal transactions. The framers deal with damages done by chattels and by human beings, thefts and other sorts of malfeasance against the property of others. The Babas in both aspects pay closest attention to how the property and person of the injured party so far as possible are restored to their prior condition, that is, a state of normality. So attention to torts focuses upon penalties paid by the malefactor to the victim, rather than upon penalties inflicted by the court on the malefactor for what he has done. When speaking of damages, the Mishnah thus takes as its principal concern the restoration of the fortune of victims of assault or robbery. Then the framers take up the complementary and corresponding set of topics, the regulation of normal transactions. When we rapidly survey the kinds of transactions of special interest, we see from the topics selected for discussion what we have already uncovered in the deepest structure of organization and articulation of the basic theme.

The other half of this same unit of three tractates presents laws governing normal and routine transactions, many of them of the same sort as those dealt with in the first half. Bailments, for example, occur in both wings of the triple tractate, first, bailments subjected to misappropriation, or accusation thereof, by the bailee, then, bailments transacted under normal circumstances. Under the rubric of routine transactions are those of workers and householders, that is, the purchase and sale of labor; rentals and bailments; real estate transactions; and inheritances and estates. Of the lot, the one involving real estate transactions is the most fully articulated and covers the widest range of problems and topics. The Babas all together thus provide a complete account of the orderly governance of balanced transactions and unchanging civil relationships within Israelite society under ordinary conditions.

The character and interests of the Division of Damages present probative evidence of the larger program of the philosophers of the Mishnah. Their intention is to create nothing less than a full-scale Israelite government, subject to the administration of sages. This government is fully supplied with a constitution and bylaws (Sanhedrin, Makkot). It makes provision for a court system and procedures (Shebuot, Sanhedrin, Makkot), as well as a full set of laws governing civil society (Baba Qamma, Baba Mesia, Baba Batra) and criminal justice (Sanhedrin, Makkot). This government, moreover, mediates between its own community and the outside (''pagan'') world. Through its system of laws it expresses its judgment of the others and at the same time defines, protects, and defends its own society and social frontiers (Abodah Zarah). It even makes provision for procedures of remission, to expiate its own errors (Horayot).

The (then-nonexistent) Israelite government imagined by the second-century philosophers centers upon the (then-nonexistent) Temple, and the (then-forbidden) city, Jerusalem. For the Temple is one principal focus. There the highest court is in session; there the high priest reigns. The penalties for law infringement are of three kinds, one of which involves sacrifice in the Temple. (The others are compensation, physical punishment, and death.) The basic conception of punishment, moreover, is that unintentional infringement of the rules of society, whether ''religious'' or otherwise, is not penalized but rather expiated through an offering in the Temple. If a member of the people of Israel intentionally infringes against the law, to be sure, that one must be removed from society and is put to death. And if there is a claim of one member of the people against another, that must be righted, so that the prior, prevailing status may be restored. So offerings in the Temple are given up to appease heaven and restore a whole bond between heaven and Israel, specifically on those occasions on which without malice or ill will an Israelite has disturbed the relationship. Israelite civil society without a Temple is not stable or normal, and not to be imagined. And the Mishnah is above all an act of imagination in defiance of reality.

The plan for the government involves a clear-cut philosophy of society, a philosophy which defines the purpose of the government and ensures that its task is not merely to perpetuate its own power. What the Israelite government, within the Mishnaic fantasy, is supposed to do is to preserve that state of perfection which, within the same fantasy, the society to begin everywhere attains and expresses. This is in at least five aspects. First of all, one of the ongoing principles of the law, expressed in one tractate after another, is that people are to follow and maintain the prevailing practice of their locale. Second, the purpose of civil penalties, as we have noted, is to restore the injured party to his prior condition, so far as this is possible, rather than merely to penalize the aggressor. Third, there is the conception of true value, meaning that a given object has an intrinsic worth, which, in the course of a transaction, must be paid. In this way the seller does not leave the transaction any richer than when he entered it, or the buyer any poorer (parallel to penalties for damages). Fourth, there can be no usury, a biblical prohibition adopted and vastly enriched in the Mishnaic thought, for money (''coins'') is what it is. Any pretense that it has become more than what it was violates, in its way, the conception of true value. Fifth, when real estate is divided, it must be done with full attention to the rights of all concerned, so that, once more, one party does not gain at the expense of the other. In these and many other aspects the law expresses its obsession with the perfect stasis of Israelite society. Its paramount purpose is in preserving and ensuring that that perfection of the division of this world is kept inviolate or restored to its true status when violated.

The Mishnah's problems are the problems of the landowner, the householder, the division's basic and recurrent subject for nearly all predicates. The Mishnah's sense of what is just and fair expresses his sense of the givenness and cosmic rightness of the present condition of society. Earth matches heaven. The Mishnah's hope for heaven and its claim on earth, to earth, corresponding to the supernatural basis for the natural world, bespeak the imagination of the surviving Israelite landowners of the mid-second-century Land of Israel. These are people deeply tired of war and its dislocation, profoundly distrustful of messiahs and their dangerous promises. They are men of substance and means, however modest, aching for a stable and predictable world in which to tend their crops and herds, feed their families and workers, keep to the natural rhythms of the seasons and the lunar cycles, and, in sum, live out their lives within strong and secure boundaries, on earth and in heaven.

That is why the sense of landed place and its limits, the sharp lines drawn between village and world, between Israelite and world, and between Temple and world evoke metaphysical correspondences which we also notice in their full expression in the Division of Appointed Times. Israel, Temple, village form a trilogy, in perfect correspondence, a deep communion. The Mishnah's deepest boundaries are locative, not utopian. These are to be preserved and defended in all of their existent, fully realized perfection. Change above all is a threat to stability and thus to perfection, to the continuity of this world of perfect correspondences between heaven and earth.

The Division of Holy Things

The Division of Holy Things presents a system of sacrifice and sanctuary; matters concerning the praxis of the altar and maintenance of the sanctuary. The praxis of the altar, specifically, involves sacrifice and things set aside for sacrifice and so deemed consecrated. The topic covers these among the eleven tractates of the present Division: Zebahim and part of Hullin, Menahot, Temurah, Keritot, part of Meilah, Tamid, and Qinnim. The maintenance of the sanctuary (inclusive of the personnel) is dealt with in Bekhorot, Arakhin, part of Meilah, Middot, and part of Hullin.

Viewed from a distance the Mishnah's tractates divide themselves up into the following groups (in parentheses are tractates containing relevant materials): (1) Rules for the altar and the praxis of the cult—Zebahim Menahot, Hullin, Keritot, Tamid, Qinnim (Bekhorot, Meilah); (2) Rules for the altar and the animals set aside for the cult—Arakhin, Temurah, Meilah (Bekhorot); and (3) Rules for the altar and support of the Temple staff and buildings—Bekhorot, Middot (Hullin, Arakhin, Meilah, Tamid). In a word, this Division speaks of the sacrificial cult and the sanctuary in which the cult is conducted. The law pays special attention to the matter of the status of the property of the altar and of the sanctuary, both materials to be utilized in the actual sacrificial rites, and property the value of which supports the cult and sanctuary in general. Both are deemed to be sanctified, that is: *qodoshim,* "holy things."

The basis of exclusion now is clear. This Division prefers not to deal with the special offerings (e.g., those designated for particular days of the week or seasons of the year), which are treated in Appointed Times; with other than animal fees for the priesthood, specifically omitting reference to agricultural dues paid over in their support, dealt with in Agriculture; or with that matrix of cleanness in which the cult is to be carried on, expounded in Purities. Those three areas of the law pertinent to the cult will at best only be alluded to here.

The inclusive principle and interests, upon closer examination, prove to be equally clear-cut and carefully defined. The matter consists of much less than everything relevant to "cult." There are decisive and pointed choices. By "holy things" we refer specifically to the altar and animals and cereals offered on the altar or belonging to the altar, and to property and goods belonging to the altar or to the sanctuary. Within these two categories we find a place for the whole of the thematic repertoire of the Fifth Division or, at the very least, account for the inclusion of each and every one of its significant topics. The Division is content to leave over for use in other Divisions materials pertinent to the altar and the sanctuary.

The system of Holy Things centers upon the everyday and rules always applicable to the cult: the daily whole offering, the sin offering and guilt offering which one may bring any time under ordinary circumstances; the right sequence of diverse offerings; the way in which the rites of the whole, sin, and guilt offerings are carried out; what sorts of animals are acceptable; the accompanying cereal offerings; the support and provision of animals for the cult and of meat for the priesthood; the support and material maintenance of the cult and its building. We have a system before us: the system of the cult of the Jerusalem Temple, seen as an ordinary and everyday affair, a continuing and routine operation. That is why special rules for the cult, both in respect to the altar and in regard to the maintenance of the buildings, personnel, and even the holy city, will be elsewhere—in Appointed Times and Agriculture. But from the perspective of Holy Things, those Divisions intersect by supplying special rules and raising extraordinary (Agriculture: land-bound; Appointed Times: time-bound) considerations for that these which Holy Things claims to set forth in its most general and unexceptional way: the cult as something permanent and everyday.

The order of Holy Things thus in a concrete way maps out the cosmology of the sanctuary and its sacrificial system, that is, the world of the Temple, which had been the cosmic center of Israelite life. A later saying states matters as follows: "Just as the navel is found at the center of a human being, so the land of Israel is found at the center of the world . . . and it is the foundation of the world. Jerusalem is at the center of the land of Israel, the Temple is at the center of Jerusalem, the Holy of Holies is at the center of the Temple, the Ark is at the

center of the Holy of Holies, and the Foundation Stone is in front of
the Ark, which spot is the foundation of the world.'' (Tanhuma Qe-
doshim 10, in Hertzberg, p. 143)

The Division of Purities

The Division of Purities presents a very simple system of three
principal parts: sources of uncleanness, objects and substances susceptible to uncleanness, and modes of purification from uncleanness. So
it tells the story of what makes what unclean and what makes it clean.
The tractates on these several topics are as follows: (1) Sources of
uncleanness—Ohalot, Negaim, Niddah, Makhshirin, Zabim, Tebul
Yom; (2) Objects and substances susceptible to uncleanness—Kelim,
Tohorot, Uqsin; and (3) Modes of purification—Parah, Miqvaot, Yadayim.

Viewed as a whole, the Division of Purities treats the interplay of
persons, food, and liquids. Dry inanimate objects or food are not
susceptible to uncleanness. What is wet is susceptible. So liquids
activate the system. What is unclean, moreover, emerges from uncleanness through the operation of liquids, specifically, through immersion in fit water of requisite volume and in natural condition.
Liquids thus deactivate the system. Thus, water in its *natural* condition
is what concludes the process by removing uncleanness. Water in its
unnatural condition, that is, deliberately affected by human agency, is
what imparts susceptibility to uncleanness to begin with. The uncleanness of persons, furthermore, is signified by body liquids or flux in the
case of the menstruating woman (Niddah) and the *zab* (Zabim). Corpse
uncleanness is conceived to be a kind of effluent, a viscous gas, which
flows like a liquid. Utensils for their part receive uncleanness when
they form receptacles able to contain liquid. In sum, we have a system
in which the invisible flow of fluidlike substances or powers serves to
put food, drink, and receptacles into the status of uncleanness and to
remove those things from that status. Whether or not we call the
system ''metaphysical,'' it certainly has no material base but is condi-
tioned upon highly abstract notions. Thus in material terms, the effect
of liquid is upon food, drink, utensils; and man. The consequences has
to do with who may eat and drink what food and liquid, and what food
and drink may be consumed in which pots and pans. These loci are
specified by tractates on utensils (Kelim) and on food and drink
(Tohorot and Uqsin).

The human being is ambivalent. That is to say, persons fall in the
middle, between sources and loci of uncleanness. They are both: they
serve as sources of uncleanness; they also become unclean. The *zab*,

the menstruating woman, the woman after childbirth, the *tebul yom*, and the person afflicted with *nega'*—all are sources of uncleanness. But being unclean, they fall within the system's loci, its program of consequences. So they make other things unclean and are subject to penalties because they *are* unclean. Unambiguous sources of uncleanness never also constitute loci affected by uncleanness. They always are unclean and never can become clean: the corpse, the dead creeping thing, and things like them. Inanimate sources of uncleanness and inanimate objects are affected by uncleanness. Systemically unique, man and liquids have the capacity to inaugurate the processes of uncleanness (as sources) and also are subject to those same processes (as objects of uncleanness). We already have considered the inner structure of this division above (pp. 70–71), so further comment is not needed.

From Description to Interpretation

The results of this protracted description of the structure and contents of the Mishnah, completed at ca. A.D. 200, may now be stated briefly and simply. It is to a situation which is so fraught with danger as to threaten the order and regularity of the stable, sacred society in its perfection and at its point of stasis that the Mishnah will devote its principal cognitive and legislative efforts. For that situation, the Mishnah will invoke heaven and express its most vivid concern for sanctification. What breaks established routine or what is broken out of established routine is what is subject to the fully articulated and extensive reflections of a whole Division of the Mishnah.

To explore the meaning of this simple result requires us now to undertake the interpretation of that which has been so painstakingly described. For that purpose one question proves critical. Since the Mishnah stands in midstream in the history of Judaism, coming as it does about seven hundred years after the redaction of the Pentateuch, we must test the possibility that the Mishnah in no way constitutes what we have claimed, namely, a systematic construction in response to the critical issues of a particular age. It may be that the Mishnah should be viewed, when seen whole, in the context not of its own time in particular but of the unfolding of the history of Scripture. For a long time the Mishnah has been seen as the formation of an essentially exegetical process. In this process it is alleged, problems of a given day were brought to Scripture and investigated in the light of the imperatives of the law of Moses. So my insistence that the Mishnah be addressed as a document of its own day, rather than as a response of its day to a document of an earlier time, requires protracted testing.

The claim was made in the behalf of the Mishnah by its earliest apologists that the document is part of the Torah of Moses, revealed by God at Mount Sinai. Now this claim, even in its mythic terms, yields two opinions on the character of the Mishnah: the Mishnah is essentially subordinate to the written Torah of Moses and is the construct of exegesis of the Pentateuchal law codes; the Mishnah is essentially autonomous of the written Torah of Moses. It is the *other* Torah, the other part of the "one whole Torah of Moses," formulated and transmitted orally from Moses' time to that of Judah the Patriarch, who is supposed to have formulated and closed the Mishnah and sponsored it as the law for Israel. Now while in a work in the history of religions, we hardly need to take up the exegesis of a theological and mythic interpretation of a principal document, in point of fact the examination of this claim concerning the definition and meaning of the Mishnah is fundamental to the problem of its interpretation. The reason is that, if the Mishnah does turn out to be essentially a secondary and contingent construct of the written Scripture, then the Mishnah cannot be placed squarely into the social context of its own time and asked to speak in particular to the political and theological crisis of the day. The Mishnah may be expected to tell us only about how the Scriptures were mediated to that day, what the meaning of the Scriptures, autonomous of the age, dictated as a message (also) to that day. In other words, the position of the Mishnah vis-à-vis that document deemed to be definitive and determinative for the Mishnah's structure and contents turns out to be critical. My approach to the interpretation of the Mishnah as a social and intellectual document rests upon my examination of that claim which the framers of the Mishnah and their heirs laid upon it to begin with, I mean, the claim that this too is *Torah*.

I shall dispose of that claim by a brief account of the facts of the relationship between Scripture and the six Divisions of the Mishnah and their various tractates. Three relationships are possible: the Mishnah depends completely on Scripture for not only facts but also basic issues; the Mishnah is completely independent of Scripture in regard to both facts and generative conceptions; and the Mishnah is partly dependent and partly independent. But since all three possible relationships can be shown to characterize the actual relationships of various tractates to the Scripture, it follows that the question has to be phrased in a different way. The matter of the relationship of the Mishnah to Scripture turns out not to be a possible point of differentiation, therefore, of definition. The taxonomic results permit no insight at all, when a document is shown to yield contradictory results. Since the Mishnah is dependent upon, and secondary to, some passages of Scripture, it is clear that close attention is paid by the Mishnah's framers to what some Scriptures have to say. But since the Mishnah is independent of other Scriptures, it is equally clear that an autonomous principle of selection of those Scriptures to receive close attention is in play. That is to say, the decision to choose one set of Scriptures and not some other is prior to the confrontation with any part of Scripture. The upshot is that the Mishnah is not simply a secondary expansion and extension of Scripture. The Mishnah is a construction, a system, formed out of an essentially independent and fresh perspective. Only after coming to full expression was it drawn to pertinent Scriptures. The Mishnah certainly can be shown to express the basic point of some passages of Scripture, to constitute an authoritative and accurate development of the meaning of selected verses in Scripture. But to understand the Mishnah we cannot turn to Scripture to begin with. The discovery and analysis of the principle of selection thus constitute a major point of differentiation, therefore of interpretation.

But the real issue is to explain the choice of those problems which determined the principle of selection in the first place. Whose problems are they? Whose questions are asked? Whose methods are used in the asking of those questions, and whose modes of thought determine the way in which problems will be phrased and solved? Thus the analysis of the substance and style, meaning and method in the document as a whole becomes the primary exercise in the interpretation of the history and structure of the Judaism framed by the Mishnah.

6

SYSTEMS AND SOURCES: THE MISHNAH AND THE TORAH OF MOSES

Why Scripture Is Critical

In the long unfolding of diverse versions of Judaism, one form of Judaism will take up and revise materials of another, existing one, dropping some available elements, adapting others, as well as inventing still others. But every sort of Judaism from the beginning of the present has had to make its peace with the Scriptures universally received as revealed by God to Moses at Mount Sinai or to the prophets, or by the "Holy Spirit" to the historians and chroniclers, psalmists and other writers. Insight into the modes and principles of selection among all these candidates for authoritative and generative status will therefore lead us far into the deepest structure and definitive tension of any given kind of Judaism. From the formation of the Pentateuch onward, framers of various sorts of Judaism have had to take measure in particular of the Mosaic revelation and lace themselves in relationship to it. Each version has found it necessary to lay claim in its own behalf to possess the sole valid interpretation of the Torah of Moses. All have alleged that they are the necessary and logical continuation of the revelation of Moses and the prophets. It is not surprising, therefore, that in behalf of the Mishnah an equivalent claim was laid down almost from the very moment of the Mishnah's completion and closure.

The diverse versions of that claim in behalf of the Mishnah indeed constitute one of the complex and interesting problems in the history of Judaism in the Mishnah's version both in the time in which the Mishnah was taking shape and afterward. But the analysis and historical evaluation of those efforts to lay down, in behalf of the Mishnah, a claim of the authority of revelation in the name of Moses and from the mouth of God just now need not detain us. The reason is that these theological formations are post facto assertions. They are not data out of the inner history of the formation of the Mishnah itself and the unfolding of its ideas. Later theologians dealt with later problems through assertions about the Mishnah's origins and Scriptural foundations. A critical question in the description and interpretation of the history of the Mishnah's version of Judaism thus is badly framed. A survey of the main versions of the later rabbinic theology of the statues of the Mishnah as coequal revelation of Moses ("Oral Torah"), therefore, at the outset is not relevant to the analysis of the evidence of the Mishnah itself. No such articulated claim is before us. Rather, it is necessary to frame the issue of the relationship of the Mishnah to Scripture in such a way as to elicit insight into the character of the Mishnah's system itself. What we want to know is what we learn about the Mishnah and the ideas of its philosophers from analysis of the relationship of the Mishnah and its corpus of themes, ideas, and facts, to the Scripture and its facts. After the facts are in hand, we may use them to interpret the Mishnah's system.

At some time it may become possible to analyze that relationship in stages, that is, the traits of the relationship between the Mishnah and Scripture before the wars, between, and after them, in sequence. For now, however, the first step in the framing of the issue is to come to the decision to deal with only the final stage in the matter, the relationship to Scripture of the Mishnah as a completed system. The reason is that, at this stage of the analysis of the unfolding of the Mishnah's ideas, our methods are not sufficiently precise and encompassing to permit us to lay claim to detailed knowledge of how things were worked out before and between the wars. The account I am able to present allows me to summarize in two sentences the state of affairs before the latter half of the second century. The framers of ideas ultimately to be located in the Mishnaic system drew heavily and informedly upon what they found in the Scriptures. But they drew upon materials they found relevant to concerns already defined, framed essentially independent of issues and themes paramount in Scripture itself. That is to say, once people had chosen a subject, they knew full well how to develop their ideas about that subject by examining and reflecting upon relevant verses of Scripture. But what dictated the choice of subject awaiting amplification and expansion was hardly a necessary or ineluctable demand of Scripture. Proof of that fact is the asymmetrical character of the interplay between the Mosaic codes and the topics developed in each of the three periods in the unfolding of the ideas of the Mishnah.

Thus, a relationship of ambiguity—freedom of choice of topic, on the one hand, disciplined literalism in working out what is to be said about a stated topic, on the other—characterizes the final product of the long period of interplay between Scripture and the philosophers of the Mishnah. That is to say, the relationship between the Mishnah and Scripture appears to be constant in the several periods of the unfolding of the Mishnah. What the philosophers of the Mishnah's ultimate system will say about any topic is, if not predictable, at least highly probable, upon the basis of what Scripture says about that same topic. But what topics the philosophers of the end product will choose for their reflection is not to be foretold on the basis of a mere reading of Scripture. At the same time, after all, that the priestly and holiness codes of Leviticus clearly appeared critical to the thinkers who lie in the remote past of the Mishnaic system of thought, to the religious imagination of the writers of the Gospels a wholly other repertoire of Scriptures obviously proved authoritative. And this is hardly surprising, for, Deuteronomy and Jeremiah came out of the same age and social setting. They are related, yet essentially in conflict with one another. Certain passages of Israelite prophecy, therefore the prophetic writings of Scripture, proved critical to the mind of people attempting to frame an account of the world formed by their encounter with Jesus. The whole corpus of prophecy and history is neglected by the Mishnah. The priestly writings of Scripture took on that same self-evidence, that same critical importance, in the mind of people, early and late; who clearly had quite profound, equivalently powerful experiences, not through the encounter with a person, self-evidently, but in the transformation effected by a world-shaping vision of sanctification.

The second step in framing the issue of the relationship of the Mishnah to Scripture is to ask what the Mishnah had to say about the meaning of the parts of Scripture the founders of the Mishnah did choose. The fact that the Mishnah constitutes a vast and detailed account of what a group of men believed Scripture to say and to mean has not been fully appreciated. The contrary polemic, that they merely repeated what they found in Scripture, has obscured their fresh results. That is to say, since it was important to apologists to show that the Mishnah constituted a contingent and dependent statement, attained through Scriptural exegesis, of what Scripture had long ago said, it has not been understood that, from a historical perspective, what we have is quite the opposite. Yet that fact is obvious and self-evident, as I shall prove. Whether or not the meaning imputed by the Mishnaic thinkers to the Scriptures is what the writers of that part of Scripture subject to exegesis wanted originally to say is not important in an understanding of the Mishnah. The fact that the Mishnaic thinkers not only selected a given topic but also framed their own ideas on that topic in response to what they found in Scripture tells us much about those ideas and that response. What we learn is how the philosophers evaluated various portions of Scripture and what they found important in them—a considerable statement.

Making Choices: Which Scriptures

It follows that we must not be taken in by the obvious links between Scripture and the Mishnah—links of theme, links of fact, links of conception. In no way may we now suppose that the Mishnah is the natural and obvious outcome of the purpose and message of scripture. That claim on the surface is spurious. For all its complete dependence upon Scripture, by its selections of themes (let alone specific verses) for amplifications and augmentation in the Mishnah, the Mishnah effects a far-reaching choice. The Mishnah constitutes a statement on the meaning Scripture, not merely a statement *of* the meaning of Scripture. For the Mishnah tells us more than what its philosophers thought important in Scripture. It also tells us how they performed remarkably sophisticated acts of logical exegesis upon the verses chosen for inquiry. The modes of thought, the concrete results, the explanation and interpretation of those results, and the reframing and fresh statement and presentation of those results in language quite independent of the modes of expression and organization of Scripture itself—recognition in detail of these achievements of insight and independent thought constitutes the greatest contribution to be made in the study of the relationship between the Mishnah and the Mosaic codes.

But there also is the fact, that much of the time the Mishnah's relationship to Scripture is not fresh and original, but subservient and literalist. The third step in the argument thus must be to point out that literalism too is not only a choice, but also a judgment upon both past and present. When the philosophers confronted the sizable heritage of Israel and made the choice to ignore most of what had been done since the time of the formation of the Mosaic codes (they would have said, at Sinai, and we know it was some six or seven hundred years before the closure of the Mishnah), they made a stunning comment. It was upon the worth and authority of what had been done in that long period separating themselves from the point in the past they chose to restate. Their judgment was that nothing of worth had happened from the time of Moses to their own day. That explains why they could ignore whatever was available in their own day and leap back to what was not. So from Scripture to their own day whatever custom or practice had come into common usage was treated as if it did not exist. This exercise in selectivity, alongside the parallel exercise in (merely) saying in their own words what already had been said in the verses chosen through the stated exercise of selectivity, constituted a program for theodicy and reform. It was more than literalism and mindless biblicism.

The point is that the Mishnah's Scriptural literalism is a response to the opening of an abyss: a bridge to the past. The Mishnah comes at the end of six or seven hundred years of history, from the time of the closure of the Torah literature at about 500 B.C. There is nothing traditional in leaping over so long a span of time. So the Mishnah's self-evident literalism when it comes to defining what is to be said about Scriptural facts is an act of reform—and therefore a disingenuous pretense. Parallel to the revival of Atticism and the idealization of the Greek past expressed in the second Sophistic, of the same time as the Mishnah, what the Mishnah does through its biblicism and literalism is to conduct a powerful polemic against folk in its own unhappy times. Its literalist traditionalism is an act of defiance, an initiative of willful consciousness.

Such a polemic, full of fresh initiatives in the utilization of ancient, but not stale, imperatives, thus is anything but traditional. It may be fairly seen as the trivialization of the past. It may not unjustly be accused of pedantry. It may reasonably be said at times to have wasted its (and our) best energies on externals. But these things, if done, were done by choice, for a purpose. The choice was not dictated by "tradition." The purpose was anything but trivial. All the minor, detailed teachings of the Mishnah, in context, address those same issues of mythological war, cosmos, and history which, in their way, others faced by going to war against the Romans and by searching for power over the rulers of this age or freedom from them. The pretense that "all we do and plan to do is merely what Scripture has said," the claim that "this time around, we shall do correctly everything the Scripture has said"—these constitute a powerful, reforming, and innovative polemic against the discredited way taken by most of their countrymen. They add up to a formidable, indeed a commanding, claim upon Israelites' attention and assent for the future.

To state the problem very simply: The superficial relationship of the Mishnah to Scripture is ambiguous only because the Mishnah never links its legal statements to Scripture or claims that it rules in accord with Scripture. On the surface, the Mishnah wishes to stand autonomous of Scripture and to claim that the source of its laws is other than Scripture. So, on first glance, the Mishnah, whatever it claims to be or to do, in no way links itself to Scripture. But, of course, hardly a second glance is needed to reveal the opposite, which is that the Mishnah depends in a deep way, for both thematic agendum and the facts of its topics and rules, upon Scripture. So, the real issue is: What are the nature of the dependence and the traits of the relationship?

The Mishnah Separate from Scripture

On the surface Scripture plays little role in the Mishnaic system. The Mishnah rarely cites a verse of Scripture, refers to Scripture as an entity, links its own ideas to those of Scripture, or lays claim to originate in what Scripture has said, even by indirect or remote allusion to a Scriptural verse of teaching. So, superficially, the Mishnah is totally indifferent to Scripture. That impression, moreover, is reinforced by the traits of the language of the Mishnah. The framers of Mishnaic discourse never attempt to imitate the language of Scripture, as do those of the Essene writings at Qumran. The very redactional structure of Scripture, found so serviceable by the writer of the Temple scroll, is of no interest whatever to the organizers of the Mishnah and its tractates, except in a few cases (Yoma, Pesahim).

I wish now to dwell on these facts. Formally, redactionally, and linguistically the Mishnah stands in splendid isolation from Scripture. This is something which had to be confronted as soon as the Mishnah came to closure and was presented as authoritative to the Jewish community of the holy Land and of Babylonia. It is not possible to point to many parallels, that is, cases of anonymous books, received as holy, in which the forms and formulations (specific verses) of Scripture play so slight a role. People who wrote holy books commonly imitated the Scripture's language; they cited concrete verses, or they claimed (at the very least) that direct revelation has come to them, as in the angelic discourses of Ezra and Baruch, so that what they say stands on an equal plane with Scripture. The internal evidence of the Mishnah's sixty-two usable tractates (excluding Abot), by contrast, in no way suggests that anyone pretended to talk like Moses and write like Moses, claimed to cite and correctly interpret things that Moses has said, or even alleged himself to have had a revelation like that of Moses and so to stand on the mountain with Moses. There is none of this. So the claim of Scriptural authority for the Mishnah's doctrines and institutions is difficult to locate within the internal evidence of the Mishnah itself.

We cannot be surprised that, in consequence of this amazing position of autonomous autocephalic authority implicit in the character of Mishnaic discourse, the Mishnah should have demanded in its own behalf some sort of apologetic. Nor are we surprised that the Mishnah attracted its share of quite hostile criticism. The issue, in the third century, would be precisely the issue phrased when we ask in general about the authority of tradition in Judaism: Why should we listen to this mostly anonymous document, which makes statements on the nature of institutions and social conduct, statements we obviously are expected to keep? Who are Meir, Yosé, Judah, Simeon, and Eleazar—

people who from the perspective of the recipients of the document, lived fifty or a hundred years ago—that we should listen to what they have to say? God revealed the Torah. Is this Mishnah too part of the Torah? If so, how? What, in other words, is the relationship of the Mishnah to Scripture, and how does the Mishnah claim authority over us such as we accord to the revelation to Moses by God at Mount Sinai? There are two important responses to the question of the place of Scripture in the Mishnaic tradition.

The Mishnah Joined to Scripture

First and most radical: the Mishnah constitutes *Torah*. It too is a statement of revelation, "Torah revealed to Moses at Sinai." But this part of revelation has come down in a form different from the well-known, written part, the Scripture. This tradition truly deserves the name "tradition," because for a long time it was handed down orally, not in writing, until given the written formulation now before us in the Mishnah. This sort of apologetic for the Mishnah appears, to begin with, in Abot, with its stunning opening chapter, linking Moses on Sinai through the ages to the earliest-named authorities of the Mishnah itself, the five pairs, on down to Shammai and Hillel. Since some of the named authorities in the chain of tradition appear throughout the materials of the Mishnah, the claim is that what these people say comes to them from Sinai through the processes of *qabbalah* and *massoret*—handing down, traditioning.

So the reason (from the perspective of the Torah myth of the Mishnah) that the Mishnah does not cite Scripture is that it does not have to. It stands on the same plane as Scripture. It enjoys the same authority as Scripture. This radical position is still more extreme than that taken by Pseudepigraphic writers, who imitate the style of Scripture, or who claim to speak within that same gift of revelation as Moses. It is one thing to say one's holy book is Scripture because it is like Scripture, or to claim that the author of the holy book has a revelation independent of that of Moses. These two positions concede to the Torah of Moses priority over their own holy books. The Mishnah's apologists make no such concession, when they allege that the Mishnah is part of the Torah of Moses. They appeal to the highest possible authority in the Israelite framework, claiming the most one can claim in behalf of the book which, in fact, bears the names of men who lived fifty years before the apologists themselves. That seems to me remarkable courage.

So that takes care of this matter of the Mishnah's not citing Scripture. When we consider the rich corpus of allusions to Scripture in other holy books, both those bearing the names of authors and those presented anonymously, we realize that the Mishnah claims its authority to be coequal with that of Scripture, while so many other holy books are made to lay claim to authority only because they depend upon the authority of Scripture and state the true meaning of Scripture. That fact brings us to the second answer to the question of the place of Scripture in the Mishnaic tradition.

The two Talmuds and the legal-exegetical writings produced in the two hundred years after the closure of the Mishnah take the position that the Mishnah is wholly dependent upon Scripture. Whatever is of worth in the Mishnah can be shown to derive directly from Scripture. So the Mishnah—tradition—is deemed distinct from, and subordinate to, Scripture. This position is expressed in an obvious way. Once the Talmuds cite a Mishnah pericope, they commonly ask, What is the source of these words? And the answer invariably is, As it is said in Scripture. This constitutes not only a powerful defense for the revealed truth of the Mishnah. For when the exegetes find themselves constrained to add proof texts from the Mishnah, they admit the need to improve and correct an existing flaw in Scripture itself.

That the search for the Scriptural bases for the Mishnah's laws constitutes both an apologetic for, and a critique of, the Mishnah is shown in the character of a correlative response to the Mishnah, namely, the Sifra and its exegesis of Leviticus (see Neusner, *Purities* VII). This rhetorical exegesis follows a standard syntactical-redactional form. Scripture will be cited. Then a statement will be made about its meaning, or a statement of law correlative to that Scripture will be given. Finally, the author of Sifra invariably states, Now is that not (merely) logical? And the point of that statement will be. Can this position not be gained through the working of mere logic, based upon facts supplied (to be sure) by Scripture? The polemical power of Sifra lies in its repetitive demonstration that the stated position—commonly, though not always, a verbatim or near-verbatim citation of a Mishnah pericope—is not only *not* the product of logic, but is, and can only be, the product of exegesis of Scripture.

What is still more to the point, that exegesis in Sifra's and the Talmud's view is formal in its character. That is, it is based upon some established mode of exegesis of the formal traits of Scriptural grammar and syntax, assigned to the remote antiquity represented by the names of Ishmael or Aqiba. So the polemic of Sifra and the Talmuds is against the positions that, first, what the Mishnah says (in the Mishnah's own words) is merely logical: and that, second, the position taken by the Mishnah can have been reached in any way other than through grammatical-syntactical exegesis of Scripture. That other way, the way of reading the Scripture through philosophical logic or practical reason, is explicitly rejected time and again. Philosophical logic is inadequate. Formal exegesis is shown to be not only adequate but necessary and indeed inexorable. It follows that Sifra undertakes to demonstrate precisely what the framers of the opening pericopes of the Talmuds' treatment of the Mishnah's successive units of thought also wish to show. The Mishnah is not autonomous. It is not independent. It is not correlative, that is, separate but equal. It is contingent, secondary, derivative, resting wholly on the foundations of the (written) revelation of God to Moses at Mount Sinai. Therein, too, lies the authority of the Mishnah as tradition.

So, there are two positions which would take shape. First, tradition in the form of the Mishnah is deemed autonomous of Scripture and enjoys the same authority as that of Scripture. The reason is that Scripture and ("oral") tradition are merely two media for conveying a single corpus of revealed law and doctrine. *Or,* tradition in the form of the Mishnah is true because it is not autonomous of Scripture. Tradition is secondary and dependent upon Scripture.

The authority of the Mishnah is the authority of Moses. That authority comes to the Mishnah directly and in an unmediated way, because the Mishnah's words were said by God to Moses at Mount Sinai and faithfully transmitted through a process of oral formulation and oral transmission from that time until those words were written down by Judah the Patriarch at the end of the second century. *Or,* that authority comes to the Mishnah indirectly, in a way mediated through the written Scriptures.

What the Mishnah says is what the Scripture says, rightly interpreted. The authority of tradition lies in its correct interpretation of the Scripture. Tradition bears no autonomous authority, is not an independent entity, and correlative with Scripture. A technology of exegesis of grammar and syntax is needed to build the bridge between tradition as contained in the Mishnah and Scripture, the original utensil shaped by God and revealed to Moses to convey the truth of revelation to the community of Israel. *Or* matters are otherwise. I hardly need to make them explicit.

The Plain Facts

First, there are tractates which simply repeat in their own words precisely what Scripture has to say, and at best serve to amplify and complete the basic ideas of Scripture. For example, all of the cultic tractates of the Second Division, the one on Appointed Times, which tell what one is supposed to do in the Temple on the various special days of the year, and the bulk of the cultic tractates of the Fifth

Division, which deal with Holy Things, simply restate facts of Scripture. For another example all of those tractates of the Sixth Division, on Purities, which specify sources of uncleanness, depend completely on information supplied by Scripture. I have demonstrated in detail that every important statement in Niddah, on menstrual uncleanness, and the most fundamental notions of Zabim, on the uncleanness of the person with flux referred to in Lev. 15, as well as every detail in Negaim, on the uncleanness of the person or house suffering the uncleanness described at Lev. 13 and 14—all of these tractates serve only to restate the basic facts of Scripture and to complement those facts with other important ones (see Neusner, *Method and Meaning II*, chapters 11, 12).

There are, second, tractates which take up facts of Scripture but work them out in a way in which those Scriptural facts cannot have led us to predict. A supposition concerning what is important *about* the facts, utterly remote from the supposition of Scripture, will explain why the Mishnah tractates under discussion say the original things they say in confronting those Scripturally provided facts. For one example, Scripture takes for granted that the red cow will be burned in a state of uncleanness, because it is burned outside the camp = Temple. The priestly writers cannot have imagined that a state of cultic cleanness was to be attained outside of the cult. The absolute datum of tractate Parah, by contrast, is that cultic cleanness not only can be attained outside of the "tent of meeting." The red cow was to be burned in a state of cleanness exceeding even that cultic cleanness required in the Temple itself. The problematic which generates the intellectual agendum of Parah, therefore, is how to work out the conduct of the rite of burning the cow in relationship to the Temple: Is it to be done in exactly the same way, or in exactly the opposite way? This mode of contrastive and analogical thinking helps us to understand the generative problematic of such tractates as Erubin and Besah, to mention only two.

And third, there are, predictably, many tractates which either take up problems in no way suggested by Scripture, or begin from facts at best merely relevant to facts of Scripture. In the former category are Tohorot, on the cleanness of foods, with its companion, Uqsin; Demai, on doubtfully tithed produce; Tamid, on the conduct of the daily whole offering; Baba Batra, on rules of real estate transactions and certain other commercial and property relationships, and so on. In the latter category are Ohalot, which spins out its strange problems with the theory that a tent and a utensil are to be compared to one another (!); Kelim, on the susceptibility to uncleanness of various sorts of utensils; Miqvaot, on the sorts of water which effect purification from uncleanness, and many others. These tractates draw on facts of Scripture. But the problems confronted in these tractates in no way respond to problems important to Scripture. What we have here is a prior program of inquiry, which will make ample provision for facts of Scripture in an inquiry to begin with generated essentially outside of the framework of Scripture.

So there we have it: some tractates merely repeat what we find in Scripture; some are totally independent of Scripture; and some fall in between. Clearly, we are no closer to a definitive answer to the question of the relationship of Scripture to the Mishnah than we were when we described the state of thought on the very same questions in the third and fourth centuries. We find everything and its opposite. But to offer a final answer to the question of Scripture-Mishnah relationships, we have to take that fact seriously. The Mishnah in no way is so remote from Scripture as its formal omission of citations of verses of Scripture suggests. In no way can it be described as contingent upon, and secondary to Scripture, as its third-century apologists claimed. But the right answer is not that it is somewhere in between. Scripture confronts the framers of the Mishnah as revelation, not merely as a source of facts. But the framers of the Mishnah had their own world with which to deal. They made statements in the framework and fellowship of their own age and generation. They were bound, therefore, to come to Scripture with a set of questions generated other than in Scripture. They brought their own ideas about what was going to be important in Scripture. This is perfectly natural.

The Meaning of the Facts

The philosophers of the Mishnah conceded to Scripture the highest authority. At the same time what they chose to hear, within the authoritative statements of Scripture, will in the end form a statement of its own. To state matters simply: all of Scripture is authoritative. But only some of Scripture is relevant. And what happened is that the framers and philosophers of the tradition of the Mishnah came to Scripture when they had reason to. That is to say, they brought to Scripture a program of questions and inquiries framed essentially among themselves. So they were highly selective. Their program itself constituted a statement *upon* the meaning of Scripture. They and their apologists of one sort hastened to add, their program consisted of a statement *of* and upon the meaning of Scripture.

In part, we must affirm the truth of that claim. When the framers of the Mishnah speak about the priestly passages of the Mosaic law codes, with deep insight they perceive profound layers of meaning embedded (''to begin with'') in those codes. What they have done with

P, moreover, they also have done, though I think less coherently, with the bulk of the Deuteronomic laws and with some of those of the Covenant Code. But their exegetical triumph—exegetical, not merely eisegetical—lies in their handling of the complex corpus of materials of the priestly code.

True, others will have selected totally different passages of Scripture, not in the Mosaic Codes to begin with. Surely we must concede that, in reading those passages, they displayed that same perspicacity as did the framers of the Mishnaic tradition who interpreted the priestly code as they did. It is in the nature of Scripture itself that such should be the case. The same Scripture which gives us the prophets gives us the Pentateuch as well—and gives priority to the Pentateuchal codes as the revelation of God to Moses.

The authority of Scripture therefore for the Mishnah is simply stated. Scripture provides indisputable facts. It is wholly authoritative—once we have made our choice of which part of Scripture we shall read. Scripture generated important and authoritative structures of the community, including disciplinary and doctrinal statements, decisions, and interpretations—once people had determined which part of Scripture to ask to provide those statements and decisions. Community structures envisaged by the Mishnah were wholly based on Scripture—when Scripture had anything to lay down. But Scripture is not wholly and exhaustively expressed in those structures which the Mishnah does borrow. Scripture has dictated the character of formative structures of the Mishnah. But the Mishnah's system is not the result of the dictation of close exegesis of Scripture—except after the fact.

These conclusions raise at the end of my description of the Mishnah precisely the question asked at the outset: How shall we account for the striking continuity from the priestly code to the Mishnah, or, to phrase matters in the current context, how shall we interpret the selections of Scriptures for exegesis made by the framers of the Mishnah? It now is appropriate to answer this question by recapitulating the principal argument offered above. The reason is that the main conclusions of the chapter to follow, and therefore of the book as a whole, about the suggestive correspondence of the social condition of Israel and the intellectual exercises of the Mishnah, rest upon the foundations outlined in the present argument. The mode of thought is the same here and in the next chapter, namely, pointing to the congruence between people's ideas and their social circumstance. The remarkable relevance to be discerned of abstract problems of thought they wished to solve to Israel's material situation of society and culture is the center of the interpretive exercise at the climax of this account of Judaism.

That is why once more we dwell on the continuity from P to the Mishnah. We see that the Mishnah takes up the perspectives of the work of the priests and Levites. We wish to account for this fact. That is, the Mishnah systematically and amply complements the priests' part of the Torah literature. It carries forward the great themes and theses of the priestly code. In theme and focus it is mainly, though not solely, a priestly document. That is why, to begin with, the Mishnah's principal themes and motifs, borrowed from the work of people of a much earlier age, have to be placed into continuity with the priestly code.

The Mishnah presents a way of organizing the world which only the priestly and other Temple castes and professions could have imagined. To point to obvious traits, we note that the document begins, in its First Division, with the claim that God owns the Land. The Land, therefore, must be used in a way consonant with the Land's holiness. More important, what the Land yields must be treated as belonging to God, until the claims of God, the landlord, have been satisfied. These claims require that the calender of the soil be set by the conduct of the cult in Jerusalem, on the one side, and that the produce of the Land be set aside for the support of the cultic castes, priests, Levites, and their dependents on the other. The document proceeds to specify the appointed times of the year, those days which are out of the ordinary. This it does by focusing upon two matters. First, the relevant appointed times, as we shall see later on, are treated principally, or solely, in terms of what is done in the cult in celebration of those special days. Second, rules governing conduct on appointed times in the towns and villages are so shaped as to bring into a single continuum of sanctification the village and the Temple. These are made into mirror images and complements of one another, so that what may be done in the Temple may not be done in the village, and vice versa. Just as the Temple is surrounded by its boundary, so the advent of the holy day causes the raising on the perimeters of the village of an invisible wall of sanctification as well. Third and fourth, two further principal Divisions of the Mishnaic system take up the matter of the conduct of the cult on ordinary days (Holy Things) and the protection of the cult from dangerous forces, understood by the Mishnaic philosophers as forces of disruption and death (Purities). All of this holds together. Uncleanness, which above all endangers the cult and must be kept away from the Temple, is what characterizes all lands but the holy Land (see Levine). The lands of the gentiles are unclean with corpse uncleanness. So death lies outside of the holy Land, with consequent uncleanness. And life lies within the holy Land, with its locus and its apogee in the Temple and at the cult.

These statements, ultimately made in the final versions of four of the six Divisions of the Mishnah, of course would not have surprised the framers of the priestly code. Indeed, as we analyzed the substantive character of the Mishnaic laws by their tractates, we found time and again that they constitute important statements not only *upon* Scripture, but also *of* what Scripture already has said. The tendency of the later Mishnaic thinkers is to amplify, expand, and extend the principles they find in the priestly code, even while these same thinkers make an original and remarkably fresh statement upon what is in the priestly code. So, in sum, there is a close continuity at the deepest layers of sentiment and opinion between the priestly code and the Mishnah. Why is it that the framers of the Mishnah chose just these cultic and priestly matters for their painstaking and detailed study? Two significant factors come into play. First, we again take account of the beginnings of the Mishnaic system. Second, we rehearse what we have already said about the fundamental ecological facts which, to begin with, are confronted by the priestly system, and which, in later times, down to the closure of the Mishnah, remained definitive of the situation of Israel. Because of the centrality of this proposition to the thesis of the book as a whole, I recapitulate the entire argument in full (see also above, pp. 17–19).

From Scripture to the Mishnah

Beginnings: As we now have seen, the Mishnaic system originates, in the century or so before 70, among either lay people who pretended to be priests, or priests who took so seriously the laws governing their cultic activity that they concluded these same laws applied even outside of the cult, or both (as in the Essene community of Qumran). When we reach the earliest possible suppositions of the earliest laws of Purities in particular, the givens of discourse turn out to maintain a closely related set of positions. First, cleanness, with special reference to food and drink, pots and pans, is possible outside of the cult. Second, cleanness is required outside of the cult. Third, the cultic taboos governing the protection and disposition of parts of the sacrificial meat which are to be given to the priests apply to other sorts of food as well. They apply, specifically, to ordinary food, not food deriving from, or related to, the altar; that is, not food directed to the priesthood. Fourth, the levitical taboos on sources of uncleanness therefore apply to ordinary food, and, it follows, fifth, one must be careful to avoid these sources of uncleanness, or to undergo a rite of purification if one has had contact with said contaminating sources. Finally, the direction and purpose of the system as a whole, in its earliest formulation, clearly are to preserve the cleanness of the people

of Israel, of the produce of the Land of Israel, of the sexual life of
Israel, of the hearth and home of Israel. So the beginnings of the
Mishnaic system lie, as I said, among lay people pretending to be
priests by eating their food at home as if they were priests in the
Temple, and also among priests with so intense a sense for cultic
cleanness that they do the same. So, in sum, at the foundations were
people who wished to act at home as if they were in the Temple, or to
pretend that they must keep purity laws at home because their home
and its life lay within the enchanted circle of the cult.

Now this position, invoking the cultic taboos for the Israelite home
and table, in fact carries forward and brings to fulfillment that priestly
position outlined in the priestly code. The social and cultural continuity
of the priestly perspective from Scripture to the Mishnah is illustrated
when its founders maintain, as they do, that the cultic laws of Leviticus
govern the Israelite table at home as much as the altar in the Temple
of Jerusalem. So I want to dwell on the matter, with special reference
to what I take to be a principal and generative rule, the taboos about
the menstruating woman's uncleanness.

When someone with the problematic of purity at home in mind
opens Scripture, his attention is drawn to the conception that cleanness
in respect to unclean bodily discharges must be kept so that the
tabernacle will be clean: "Thus you shall keep the people of Israel
separate from their uncleanness, lest they die in their uncleanness by
defiling my tabernacle that is in their midst" (Lev. 15:31). But the
menstruant, *zab, zabah,* and woman after childbirth do not go to the
Temple. The priestly code is explicit that a rite of purification must be
undertaken by the last three named (Lev. 15:13–15 for the *zab,* Lev.
15:28–30 for the *zabah,* and Lev. 12:6–8 for the woman after childbirth). Accordingly, someone reading the Scripture will have asked
himself, How are the unclean people going to make the Temple
unclean, when, in point of fact, before they are able to enter its
precincts, they undergo the rite of purification Scripture itself speci-
fies? And, he will have answered. The people of Israel itself, *in whose
midst is the tabernacle,* is to be kept clean, so that the tabernacle,
which is in their midst, will be in a clean setting. It will follow that the
rules of cleanness in general pertaining to the Temple must apply as
well to the people outside of the Temple.

The rules of menstrual uncleanness and comparable uncleanness in
the beginning, before the revision accomplished by P in the sixth or
fifth century, had nothing to do with the cult. Menstrual taboos are not
associated with the cult even in the very pericopes of the priestly code
which refer to them. It is only in the subscription (Lev. 15:31) that the
priestly code naturally insists upon an integral and necessary relationship between menstrual taboos and the cult, and this, as I said, is even

redactionally claimed only after the fact. We assume that everyone avoided having sexual relations with menstruating women, without regard to whether or not he intended to go to the Temple, indeed to whether or not he even lived in the Land of Israel. Land, people, Temple—all form an integrated and whole realm of being, to be kept clean so as to serve as the locus of the sacred. Israel must be clean because of the tabernacle in their midst. Because the tabernacle is in their midst, Israel must be clean, even when not in the tabernacle, which is exactly what Lev. 15:31 says—to someone who to begin with thought so.

Ecology: The exclusiveness which constituted the response of priests and the followers of Ezra and Nehemiah to the critical problems of Israelite self-definition in the sixth and fifth centuries because of continuing political and social changes remained a pressing problem for the next six or seven hundred years. When we find that a formative group in Israelite society retained the fundamental perspectives and even the detailed laws which took shape to make a statement upon the definition of Israel in that one situation, we are on solid ground in asking whether the reason may be that the situation remained essentially the same. The perennial dilemmas endured fundamentally unchanged, long afterward. Obviously, much that was new entered the Israelite social and political framework. Yet what we are constrained to call "Hellenization," meaning an epoch of internationalization and open borders, a cosmopolitan age of swiftly flowing currents in culture and thought, an era in which a common cosmopolitan culture spread throughout the great empire of the Mediterranean basin, expressed, to be sure, in an idiom distinctive to one group or some other—that "Hellenization" (I should prefer: *modernization*) remained a fact of life.

For from the moment at which trade and commerce in goods and ideas broke down walls of isolation of one group from another, one region from another, the issue of who each group was, and what each group might claim for its own self-definition in order to explain its distinctive existence, proved pressing. What was now needed was walls of another sort. No one now had to ask about what one group shared in common with all others. That was no issue. The answers in the cosmopolitan culture and economy were obvious. In the special case of Israel in the Land of Israel, moreover, the dispersion among gentiles within the holy Land, the absence of contiguous settlement, the constant confrontation with other languages and other ways of life along with the preposterous claims of Scripture that Israel alone owned the Land, and Israel's God alone owned the world—these dissonances between social reality and imaginative fantasy raised to a point of acute concern what was in other settings a merely chronic and ongoing perplexity.

Now when we ask why the Temple with its cult enduringly proved central in the imagination of the Israelites in the country, as indeed it was, we have only to repeat the statements which the priests of the Temple and their imitators in the sects were prepared to make. These explain the critical importance of cult and rite. The altar was the center of life, the conduit of life from heaven to earth and from earth to heaven. All things are to be arrayed in relationship to the altar. The movement of the heavens demarcated and celebrated at the cult marked out the divisions of time in relationship to the altar. The spatial dimension of the Land was likewise demarcated and celebrated in relationship to the altar. The natural life of Israel's fields and corrals, the social life of its hierarchical caste-system, the political life (this was not only in theory by any means) centered on the Temple as the locus of ongoing government—all things in order and in place expressed the single message. The natural order of the world corresponded to, reinforced, and was reinforced by, the social order of Israel. Both were fully realized in the cult, the nexus between those opposite and corresponding forces, the heavens and the earth.

The lines of structure emanated from the altar. And it was these lines of structure which constituted these high and impenetrable frontiers which separated from the gentiles Israel, which was holy, ate holy food, reproduced itself in accord with the laws of holiness, and conducted all of its affairs, both affairs of state and the business of the table and the bed, in accord with the demands of holiness. So the cult defined holiness. Holiness meant separateness. Separateness meant life. Why? Because outside of the Land, the realm of the holy, lay the domain of death. The lands are unclean. The Land is holy. For the Scriptural vocabulary, one antonym for *holy* is *unclean,* and one opposite of unclean is holy. The synonym of holy is life. The principal force and symbol of uncleanness and its highest expression are death.

That is why cult plays so critical a role in the self-definition of Israel, as both the priestly and holiness codes and the Mishnah at its beginnings wish to express what makes Israel distinct and distinctive. Their message is one of metaphysics. But it can be stated as a judgment upon society as well: if the people is to live, it must be as a holy people. Imitating the holy God it must be wholly other, wholly different, set apart from the unclean lands of death on earth, just as God is set apart from the no-gods in heaven. What has been said renders vivid the issue confronting the continuators of the Mishnaic work: the people who had witnessed the destruction of the Temple. It is one thing when the Temple is standing to pretend to be priests and to eat like the priests and like God in the cult. It is quite another to do so amid the Temple's rubble and ruins, and in the certainty that those who did the work would not live to see the Temple they were planning and to celebrate the perfection of creation at the altar.

7

JUDAISM:
THE EVIDENCE OF THE MISHNAH

The Social Description of the Mishnah

The Judaism shaped by the Mishnah consists of a coherent world view and comprehensive way of living. It is a world view which speaks of transcendent things, a way of life in response to the supernatural meaning of what is done, a heightened and deepened perception of the sanctification of Israel in deed and in deliberation. Sanctification means two things, first, distinguishing Israel in all its dimensions from the world in all its ways; second, establishing the stability, order, regularity, predictability, and reliability of Israel at moments and in contexts of danger. Danger means instability, disorder, irregularity, uncertainty, and betrayal. Each topic of the system as a whole takes up a critical and indispensable moment or context of social being. Through what is said in regard to each of the Mishnah's principal topics, what the system as a whole wishes to declare is fully expressed. Yet if the parts severally and jointly give the message of the whole, the whole cannot exist without all of the parts, so well joined and carefully crafted are they all.

The critical issue in economic life, which means, in farming, is in two parts.

First, Israel, as tenant on God's holy land, maintains the property in the ways God requires, keeping the rules which mark the Land and its crops as holy. Next, the hour at which the sanctification of the Land comes to form a critical mass, namely, in the ripened crops, is the moment ponderous with danger and heightened holiness. Israel's will so affects the crops as to mark a part of them as holy, the rest of them as available from common use. The human will is determinative in the process of sanctification.

Second, what happens in the Land at certain times, at "appointed times," marks off spaces of the Land as holy in yet another way. The center of the Land and the focus of its sanctification is the Temple. There the produce of the Land is received and given back to God, the one who created and sanctified the Land. At these unusual moments of sanctification, the inhabitants of the Land in their social being in villages enter a state of spatial sanctification. That is to say, the village boundaries mark off holy space.

This is expressed in two ways. First, the Temple itself observes and expresses the special, recurring holy time. Second, the villages of the Land are brought into alignment with the Temple, forming a complement and completion to the Temple's sacred being. The advent of the appointed times precipitates a spatial reordering of the Land, so that the boundaries of the sacred are matched and mirrored in village and in Temple. At the heightened holiness marked by these moments of appointed times, therefore, the occasion for an effective sanctification is worked out. Like the harvest, the advent of an appointed time such as a pilgrim festival is also a sacred season and is made to express that regular, orderly, and predictable sort of sanctification for Israel which the system as a whole seeks.

If we now leap over the next two divisions, we come to the counterpart of the Divisions of Agriculture and Appointed Times, Holy Things and Purities, namely, dealing with the everyday and the ordinary, as against the special moments of harvest, on the one side, and special time or season, on the other. Here what is to be said hardly needs specification. The Temple, the locus of sanctification, is conducted in a wholly routine and trustworthy, punctilious manner. The one thing which may unsettle matters is the intention and will of the human actor. This is subjected to carefully prescribed limitations and remedies. The Division of Holy Things generates its companion, the one on cultic cleanness, Purities. The relationship between the two is like that between Agriculture and Appointed Times, the former locative, the latter utopian, the former dealing with the fields, the latter with the interplay between fields and altar. Here, too, once we speak of the one place of the Temple, we address, too, the cleanness which pertains to every place. A system of cleanness, taking into account what imparts uncleanness and how this is done, what is subject to uncleanness, and how that state is overcome—that system is fully expressed, once more, in response to the participation of the human will. Without the wish and act of a human being, the system does not function. It is inert. Sources of uncleanness, which come naturally and not by volition, and modes of purification, which work naturally and not by human intervention, remain inert until human will has imparted susceptibility to uncleanness, that is, introduced into the system food and drink, bed, pot, chair, and pan, which to begin with form the focus of the system. The movement from sanctification to uncleanness takes place when human will and work precipitate it.

The middle Divisions, the Third and Fourth, on Women and Damages, finally, take their place in the structure of the whole by showing the congruence, within the larger framework of regularity and order, of human concerns of family and farm, politics and workaday transactions among ordinary people. For without attending to these matters, the Mishnah's system does not encompass what, at its foundations, it is meant to comprehend and order. So what is at issue is fully cogent with the rest. In the case of Women, attention focuses upon the point of disorder marked by the transfer of that disordering anomaly, woman, from the regular status provided by one man, to the equally trustworthy status provided by another. That is the point at which the Mishnah's interests are aroused: once more, predictably, the moment of disorder. In the case of Damages, there are two important concerns. First, there is the paramount interest in preventing, so far as possible, the disorderly rise of one person and fall of another, and in sustaining the status quo of the economy of Israel, the holy society in stasis. Second, there is the necessary concomitant in the provision of a system of political institutions to carry out the laws which preserve the balance and steady state of persons.

The two Divisions which take up topics of concrete and material concern, the formation and dissolution of families and the transfer of property in that connection, the transactions, both through torts and through commerce, which lead to exchanges of property and the potential dislocation of the state of families in society, are locative and utopian at the same time. They deal with the concrete locations in which people make their lives, household and street and field, the sexual and commercial exchanges of a given village. But they pertain to the life of all Israel, both in the Land and otherwise. These two Divisions, together with the household ones of Appointed Times, constitute the sole opening outward toward the life of utopian Israel, that diaspora in the far reaches of the ancient world, in the endless span of time. This community from the Mishnah's perspective is not only in exile but unaccounted for, outside the system, for the Mishnah declines to recognize it and take it into account. Israelites who dwell in the land of (unclean) death instead of in the Land simply fall outside of the range of (holy) life.

To Whom the Mishnah Speaks

Now if we ask ourselves about the sponsorship and source of special interest in the topics just now reviewed, we shall come up with obvious answers.

In so far as the Mishnah is a document about the holiness of Israel in its Land, it expresses that conception of sanctification and theory of its modes which will have been shaped among those to whom the Temple and its technology of joining heaven and holy Land through the sacred place defined the core of being, I mean, the caste of the priests.

In so far as the Mishnah takes up the way in which transactions are conducted among ordinary folk and takes the position that it is through documents that transactions are embodied and expressed (surely the position of the relevant tractates on both Women and Damages), the Mishnah expresses what is self-evident to scribes. Just as, to the priest, there is a correspondence between the table of the Lord in the Temple and the locus of the divinity in the heavens, so, to the scribe, there is a correspondence between the documentary expression of the human will on earth, in writs of all sorts, in the orderly provision of courts for the predictable and just disposition of exchanges of persons and property, and heaven's judgment of these same matters. When a woman becomes sanctified to a particular man on earth, through the appropriate document governing the transfer of her person and property, in heaven as well, the woman is deemed truly sanctified to that man. A violation of the writ therefore is not merely a crime. It is a sin. That is why the Temple rite involving the wife accused of adultery is integral to the system of the Division of Women.

So there are these two social groups, not categorically symmetrical with one another, the priestly caste and the scribal profession, for whom the Mishnah makes self-evident statements. We know, moreover, that in time to come, the scribal profession would become a focus of sanctification too. The scribe would be transformed into the rabbi, locus of the holy through what he knew, just as the priest had been, and would remain locus of the holy through what he could claim for genealogy. The tractates of special interest to scribes-become-rabbis and to their governance of Israelite society, those of Women and Damages, together with certain others particularly relevant to utopian Israel beyond the system of the Land—those tractates would grow and grow. Others would remain essentially as they were with the closure of the Mishnah. So we must notice that the Mishnah, for its part, speaks for the program of topics important to the priests. It takes up the persona of the scribes, speaking through their voice and in their manner.

Now what we do not find, which becomes astonishing in the light of these observations, is sustained and serious attention to the matter of the caste of the priests and of the profession of the scribes. True, scattered through the tractates are exercises, occasionally sustained and important exercises, on the genealogy of the priestly caste, upon their marital obligations and duties, as well as on the things priests do and do not do in the cult, in collecting and eating their sanctified food, and in other topics of keen interest to priests. Indeed, it would be no exaggeration to say that the Mishnah's system seen whole is not a great deal more than a handbook of how the priestly caste wished to design its life in Israel and the world. And yet in the fundamental structure of the document, its organization into Divisions and tractates, there is no place for a Division of the Priesthood, no room even for a complete tractate on the rules of the priesthood, except, as we have seen, for the pervasive way of life of the priestly caste, which is everywhere. This absence of sustained attention to the priesthood is striking, when we compare the way in which the priestly code at Lev. 1–15 spells out its concerns: the priesthood, the cult, the matter of cultic cleanness. Since we have Divisions for the cult and for cleanness at Holy Things and Purities, we are struck that we do not have this Third Division.

We must, moreover, be equally surprised that, for a document so rich in the importance lent to petty matters of how a writ is folded and where the witnesses sign, so obsessed with the making of long lists and the organization of all knowledge into neat piles of symmetrically arranged words, the scribes who know how to make lists and match words nowhere come to the fore. They speak through the document. But they stand behind the curtains. They write the script, arrange the sets, design the costumes, situate the players in their place on the stage, raise the curtain—and play no role at all. We have no Division or tractate on such matters as how a person becomes a scribe, how a scribe conducts his work, who forms the center of the scribal profession and how authority is gained therein, the rights and place of the scribe in the system of governance through courts, the organization and conduct of schools or circles of masters and disciples through which the scribal arts are taught and perpetuated. This absence of even minimal information on the way in which the scribal profession takes shape and does its work is stunning when we realize that, within a brief generation, the Mishnah as a whole would fall into the hands of scribes, to be called rabbis, both in the Land of Israel and in Babylonia. These rabbis would make of the Mishnah exactly what they wished. Construed from the perspective of the makers of the Mishnah, the priests and the scribes who provide contents and form, substance and style, therefore, the Mishnah turns out to omit all reference to actors, when laying out the world which is their play.

The metaphor of the theater for the economy of Israel, the household of holy Land and people, space and time, cult and home, leads to yet another perspective. When we look out upon the vast drama portrayed by the Mishnah, lacking as it does an account of the one who wrote the book, and the one about whom the book was written, we notice yet one more missing component. In the fundamental and generative structure of the Mishnah, we find no account of that other necessary constituent: the audience. To whom the document speaks is never specified. What group ("class") generates the Mishnah's problems is not at issue. True, it is taken for granted that the world of the Mishnah expresses the sanctified being of Israel in general. So the Mishnah speaks about the generality of Israel, the people. But to whom, within Israel, the Mishnah addresses itself, and what groups are expected to want to know what the Mishnah has to say, are matters which never come to full expression.

Yet there can be no doubt of the answer to the question. The building block of Mishnaic discourse, the circumstance addressed whenever the issues of concrete society and material transactions are taken up, is the householder and his context. The Mishnah knows about all sorts of economic activities. But for the Mishnah the center and focus of interest lie in the village. The village is made up of households, each a unit of production in farming. The households are constructed by, and around, the householder, father of an extended family, including his sons and their wives and children, his servants, his slaves, the craftsmen to whom he entrusts tasks he does not choose to do. The concerns of householders are in transactions in land. Their measurement of value is expressed in acreage of top, middle, and bottom grade. Through real estate critical transactions are worked out. The marriage settlement depends upon real property. Civil penalties are exacted through payment of real property. The principal transactions to be taken up are those of the householder who owns beasts which do damage or suffer it; who harvests his crops and must set aside and so by his own word and deed sanctify them for use by the castes scheduled from on high; who uses or sells his crops and feeds his family; and who, if he is fortunate, will acquire still more land. It is to householders that the Mishnah is addressed: the pivot of society and its bulwark, the units of which the village is composed, the corporate component of the society of Israel in the limits of the village and the Land. The householder, as I said, is the building block of the house of Israel, of its *economy* in the classic sense of the word.

So, to revert to the metaphor which has served us well, the great proscenium constructed by the Mishnah now looms before us. Its arch is the canopy of heaven. Its stage is the holy Land of Israel. Its actors are the holy people of Israel. Its events are the drama of unfolding time and common transactions, appointed times and holy events. Yet in this grand design we look in vain for the three principal participants: the audience, the actors, and the playwright. So we must ask why.

The reason is not difficult to discover, when we recall that, after all, what the Mishnah really wants is for nothing to happen. The Mishnah presents a tableau, a wax museum, a diorama. It portrays a world fully perfected and so fully at rest. The one thing the Mishnah does not want to tell us is about change, how things come to be what they are. That is why there can be no sustained attention to the priesthood and its rules, the scribal profession and its constitution, the class of householders and its interests. The Mishnah's pretense is that all of these have come to rest. They compose a world in stasis, perfect and complete, made holy because it is complete and perfect. It is an economy—again in the classic sense of the word—awaiting the divine *act* of sanctification which, as at the creation of the world, would set the seal of holy rest upon an again-complete creation, just as in the beginning. There is no place for the actors when what is besought is no action whatsoever, but only perfection, which is unchanging. There is room only for a description of how things are: the present tense, the sequence of completed statements and static problems. All the action lies within, in how these statements are made. Once they come to full expression, with nothing left to say, there also is nothing left to do, no need for actors, whether scribes, priests, or householders.

What makes up a world view and way of life are the people who see the world in one particular way and expect to live in accord with a way of living congruent with that singular world view. So the components of the system at the very basis of things are the social groups to whom the system refers. These groups obviously are not comparable to one another. As the framers of Kilayim and Nedarim would notice, they are not three species of the same social genus. One is a caste; the second, a profession; the third, a class. What they have in common is, first, that they do form groups; and, second, that the groups are social in foundation and collective in expression. That is not a sizable claim. The priesthood is a social group; it coalesces. Priests see one another as part of a single caste, with whom, for example, they will want to intermarry. The scribes are a social group, because they practice a single profession, following a uniform set of rules. They coalesce in the methods by which they do their work. The householders are a social group, the basic productive unit of society, around which other economic activity is perceived to function. In an essentially agricultural economy, it is quite reasonable to regard the householder, the head of a basic unit of production, as part of a single class.

The Mishnah in form, function, and fact is one book, one cogent system. All of its parts interact with all others. That proposition has been the labor and the burden of the sustained account of chapter 4, above. As a single system, the Mishnah reveals the operation of a single principle of selection. That was the argument of chapter 6 in which the autonomy and inner cogency of the Mishnah were demonstrated through the exercise of differentiation made possible by a single point of reference, the relationship to Scripture and its authority. Once we saw that the Mishnah does not fall into place as a secondary expansion of the Scripture, we could perceive clearly that the Mishnah does coalesce and find cogency through its distinctive principle of selection of those Scriptures which were deemed useful and serviceable in the work defined, to begin with, by the framers of the Mishnah themselves. So, as is clear, and as has been asserted from the opening lines of this book, the Mishnah presents a system, distinctive, whole, fully interacting in all of its parts, capable of making a coherent statement. True, that statement expresses the viewpoints of diverse social groups. But it is one statement, made to a single world in behalf of a single world. That is why the Mishnah coalesces. In this chapter I claim to make that statement, both in its form and in its substance.

This also is why the Mishnah would fall to pieces nearly as soon as it did come together. For that world to which the Mishnah spoke was not a single world at all. The social coalition for which, at a single, enchanted moment, the Mishnah spoke, and to which, for an hour of sustained attention, the Mishnah would address its message, would be a heap of ruins before the play (which was to have no action or plot) was over.

What Makes the Mishnah Mishnaic

Now this second task, subjected to so long an introduction, may be briefly stated. We have to ask how the several perspectives joined in the Mishnah do coalesce. What that single message is which brings them all together, and how that message forms a powerful, if transient, catalyst for the social groups which hold it—these define the final task in portraying the Judaism for which the Mishnah is the whole evidence. Integral to that task, to be sure, is an account of why, for the moment, the catalyst could serve, as it clearly did, to join together diverse agents, to mingle, mix, indeed unite, for a fleeting moment, social elements quite unlike one another, indeed not even capable of serving as analogies for one another.

As we shall see in due course, one of the recurring exercises of the Mishnaic thinkers is to give an account of how things which are different from one another become part of one another, that is, the problem of mixtures. This problem of mixtures will be in many dimensions, involving cases of doubt; cases of shared traits and distinctive ones; cases of confusion of essentially distinct elements and components; and numerous other concrete instances of successful and of unsuccessful, complete and partial catalysis. If I had to choose one prevailing motif of Mishnaic thought, it is this: the joining together of categories which are distinct. The Mishnaic mode of thought is to bring together principles and to show both how they conflict and how the conflict is resolved; to deal with gray areas and to lay down principles for disposing of cases of doubt; to take up the analysis of entities into their component parts and the catalysis of distinct substances into a single entity; to analyze the whole, then synthesize the parts. The motive force behind the Mishnah's intellectual program of cases and examples, the thing the Mishnah wants to do with all of the facts it has in its hand, is described within this inquiry into mixtures. Now the reasons for this deeply typical, intellectual concern with confusion and order, I think, are probably to be found here and there and everywhere.

For, after all, the basic mode of thought of the priests who made up the priestly creation legend is that creation is effected through the orderly formation of each thing after its kind and correct location of each in its place. The persistent quest of the Mishnaic subsystems is for stasis, order, the appropriate situation of all things.

A recurrent theme in the philosophical tradition of Greco-Roman antiquity, current in the time of the Mishnah's formative intellectual processes, is the nature of mixtures, the interpenetration of distinct substances and their qualities, the juxtaposition of incomparables (see Sambursky and Neusner, *Purities* XII, pp. 206–9). The types of mixtures were themselves organized in a taxonomy: a mechanical composition, in which the components remain essentially unchanged, a total fusion, in which all particles are changed and lose their individual properties, and, in between, a mixture proper, in which there is a blending. So concern for keeping things straight and in their place is part of the priestly heritage. Perhaps it was also familiar to the philosophical context of scribes; that is far less certain. Householders can well have understood the notion of well-marked borders and stable and dependable frontiers between frontiers between different properties. What was to be fenced in and fenced out hardly requires specification.

And yet, however tradition and circumstance may have dictated this point of interest in mixtures and their properties, in sorting out what is confused and finding a proper place for every thing, I think there is still another reason for the recurrence of a single type of exercise and a uniform mode of thought. It is the social foundation for the intellectual exercise which is the Mishnah and its Judaism. In my view the very condition of Israel, standing, at the end of the second century, at the end of its own history, at the frontiers among diverse peoples, on both sides of every boundary, whether political or cultural or intellectual—it is the condition of Israel itself which attracted attention to this matter of sorting things out. The concern for the catalyst which joins what is originally distinct, the powerful attraction of problems of confusion and chaos, on the one side, and order and form, on the other—these form the generative problematic of the Mishnah as a system because they express in intellectual form the very nature and being of Israel in its social condition. It is therefore the profound congruence of the intellectual program and the social realities taken up and worked out by that intellectual program which both accounts for the power of the Mishnah to define the subsequent history of Judaism and justifies calling the Mishnah an expression and form of Judaism. The joining together of these distinct forces for order—caste, profession, class—forms the final stage in the description and interpretation of the Mishnah's kind of Judaism. That Judaism, at its deepest foundations, is the creation and expression of the catalyst which joins and holds the parts together.

The Nature of Mixtures

Let us take up, first of all, the matter of style: the things the Mishnah wants to *do* with the points of interest, topics of concern, and, above all, sheer volume of facts which flow into the Mishnah from the Scriptures chosen for exegesis and from diverse other sources, literary and societal. In the next unit we take up that perspective on all things which corresponds to this distinctive style: the things the Mishnah wants to say about the facts, the message the Mishnah frames through the medium of facts and the exegesis of them. This medium and message, corresponding to one another, we shall see, define what is particular to the Mishnah, distinct from any one of its components' messages. The Mishnah adds up to much more than the sum of its three principal parts. There are both a mode of thought and a particular message which make the Mishnah coherent and distinctive, not merely the construct of priests, scribes, or householders. The former is now to be described and catalogued.

Gray Areas of the Law

Nearly all disputes which dominate and characterize the rhetoric of the Mishnah derive from bringing diverse legal principles into juxtaposition and conflict. So we may say that the Mishnah as a whole is an exercise in the application to a given case, through practical and applied reason, of several distinct principles of law. In this context, it follows, the Mishnah is a protracted inquiry into the intersection of principles; it maps out the gray areas of the law delimited by such confused borders. An example of this type of "mixture" of legal principles comes in the conflict of two distinct bodies of the law, for instance, the requirement to circumcise on the eighth day, even when this is the Sabbath (M. Shab. 19:1ff.), the requirement to kill and roast the Passover offering on the fourteenth of Nisan, even when this is the Sabbath (M. Pes. 6:1ff.), and the like. Yet another conflict of rules demanding resolution is a case in which a high priest and a Nazirite, both of them prohibited from contracting corpse uncleanness, come upon a neglected corpse, which one of them must bury (M. Naz. 7:1).

But gray areas are discerned not only through mechanical juxtaposition, through making up a conundrum of distinct principles of law. On the contrary, the Mishnaic philosophers are at their best when they force into conflict laws which, to begin with, scarcely intersect. This they do, for example, by inventing cases in which the secondary implications of one law are brought into conflict with the secondary implications of some other. An excellent example of the Mishnah's power on its own to discern (or invent) a gray area of law and to explore its logic is to be located in the issue of the effect of removing heave offering from produce which the householder is not yet obliged to tithe. Normally, we know, heave offering is removed from produce which is forbidden for use until the heave offering is taken out. But this produce under discussion is not yet forbidden. That is, it has not yet entered that status in which use is not allowed until heave offering is removed. The produce presently is exempt from the law. So the issue is whether the act of removing the heave offering from said produce imposes upon the produce a status which otherwise it would not receive (M. Ma. 2:4).

Excluded Middles

A species of the genus of gray areas of the law is the excluded middle, that is, that creature or substance which appears to fall between two distinct and definitive categories. The Mishnah's framers time and again allude to or even invent such an entity, because it forms the excluded middle which inevitably will attract attention and demand categorization. There are types of recurrent middles among both human beings and animals as well as vegetables. Indeed, the obsession with the excluded middle leads the Mishnah to invent its own examples, which have then to be analyzed into their definitive components and situated in their appropriate category. What this does is to leave no area lacking in an appropriate location, none to yield irresolvable doubt. An example of the exercise of making up a problem for solution and then solving it is the townsman who goes to a village, or villager who goes to a town. Each is subject to his own rule, e.g., for the date of reading the Scroll of Esther, and what each is to do when in another location has to be properly settled (M. Meg. 2:3).

The purpose of identifying the excluded middle, of course, is to allow the lawyers to sort out distinct rules, on the one side, and to demonstrate how they intersect without generating intolerable uncertainty, on the other. For example, to explore the theory that an object can serve as either a utensil or a tent, that is, a place capable of spreading the uncleanness of a corpse under its roof, the framers of the Mishnah invent a hive. This is sufficiently large so that it can be imagined to be either a utensil or a tent. When it is whole, it is the former, and if it is broken, it is the latter. The location of the object, e.g., on the ground, off the ground, in a doorway, against a wall, and so on, will further shape the rules governing the cases (M. Oh. 9:1–14; cf. M. Kel. 8:1ff). Again, to indicate the ambiguities lying at the frontiers, the topic of the status of Syria will come under repeated discussion. Syria is deemed not wholly sanctified, as is the Land of Israel, but also not wholly outside of the frame of holy Land, as are all other countries. That is why to Syria apply some rules applicable to holy Land, and some rules applicable to secular land. In consequence, numerous points of ambiguity will be uncovered and explored (see M. Sheb. 6:1–6). One example is this: if a field in Syria is adjacent to the Land of Israel and can be reached without contamination, it is deemed part of the Land. If not, it is deemed unclean but is still liable to the laws of tithes and the seventh year (M. Oh. 18:7).

Types of Mixtures

Gray areas of the law in general, and the excluded middle in particular, cover the surface of the law. They fill up nearly every chapter of the Mishnah. But underneath the surface is an inquiry of profound and far-reaching range. It is into the metaphysical or philosophical issues of how things join together and how they do not, of synthesis and analysis, of fusion and union, connection, division, and disintegration. What we have in the recurrent study of the nature of mixtures, broadly construed, is a sustained philosophical treatise in the guise of an episodic exercise in ad hoc problem solving. It is as if the cultic agendum laid forth by the priests, the social agendum defined by the confusing status and condition of Israel, and the program for right categorization of persons and things set forth for the scribes to carry out—all were taken over and subsumed by philosophers who proposed to talk abstractly about what they deemed urgent, while using the concrete language and syntax of other sorts of minds. To put it differently, the framers of the Mishnah, in their reflection on the nature of mixtures in their various potentialities for formation and dissolution, shape the topics provided by others into hidden discourse on an encompassing philosophical-physical problem of their own choosing.

In so doing, as we shall see in the final sections, they phrased the critical question demanding attention and response, the question at once social, political, metaphysical, cultural, and even linguistic, but above all, historical: the question of Israel standing at the outer boundaries of a long history now decisively done with. That same question of acculturation and assimilation, alienation and exile, which had confronted the priests of old is raised once more. Now it is framed in terms of mechanical composition, fusion, and something in between, mixture. But it is phrased in incredible terms of a wildly irrelevant world of unseen things, of how we define the place of the stem in the entity of the apple, the effect of the gravy upon the meat, and the definitive power of a bit of linen in a fabric of wool. In concrete form, the issues are close to comic. In abstract form, the answers speak of nothing of workaday meaning. In reality, at issue is Israel in its Land, once the lines of structure which had emanated from the Temple had been blurred and obliterated.

To begin with, there are certain general propositions governing all cases of mixtures. These may be expressed through particulars of the law, but appear throughout the law. For example, the theory of mixtures distinguishes between mixtures of the same species and those of different ones. When the same species are mixed, they are assumed to be fully uniform. When different species are mixed, there must be some evidence that one kind has imparted its traits to the other kind, before the status of the former is deemed to affect that of the latter (M. A.Z. 5:8). The notion that the categories of creation must be kept orderly and distinct is expressed in the principle that one may not separate heave offering from one batch of produce in behalf of a batch of produce of a different sort. Diverse species of produce must be kept distinct from one another (M. Ter. 2:4). On the other hand, if there is a large batch of produce of a single kind, then one may separate the part of that produce which is of the highest quality to cover the whole batch of produce. Whether or not diverse substances join together to form the volume requisite to constitute a violation of the law is a repeated exercise in the theory of mixtures. This same matter of joining together also is affected by deeds. If we have an improper intention to do one thing to half of the requisite volume of a substance, and an improper intention to do some other thing with the other half of the requisite volume, that is null, "for eating and offering up do not join together" (M. Zeb. 6:7). Where we have two fabrics, one in one category of susceptibility to uncleanness, another in a different category (e.g., one deemed susceptible at a small size, another at a larger size), then the degree of susceptibility applicable to the more stringent of the two pieces is the one which applies. If the material added is subject to greater restriction, then that restriction applies to the whole (M. Kel. 27:3).

The basic possibilities are two. One substance may be deemed fully to join together with, and form an integral part of, another. Or two substances may be deemed essentially separate from one another. Now these two possibilities may be shown to inhere not only in substances, but also in deeds, among persons, and in all manner of social circumstances. For example, we may take up a mixture of actions and ask whether they all constitute a single, extended deed, culpable only on one count, or many discrete deeds, each of them subject to punishment. The ambiguity of determining when an action is single and complete, and when it forms part of a sequence of actions, all of them deemed to constitute a single action for the purpose of the law, is frequently explored. One instance is whether one has to cover up one time or many times the blood of a hundred beasts which one has slaughtered in a single location. Another treats bringing one offering for many sinful acts, or many offerings for one sinful act (M. Hul. 6:4; M. Ker. 1:7, 2:3–6, 3:2–3, 4–6, etc.).

When, finally, we have a mixture which produces total confusion, we must take account of all possibilities. This sort of mixture forms the bridge to the principles of the resolution of doubts, since, we observe, where we do not know the traits of the components of a mixture and therefore cannot be sure whether the status of one component has or has not affected that of others, we have to treat the mixture as a matter of doubt. For example, if a person convicted of murder is confused with others, all are exempt from the death penalty. If various people convicted of the death penalty are confused, so that the form of the death penalty appropriate to this one cannot be distinguished from the form of the death penalty applying to some other, the most lenient mode of execution is applied to all of them (M. San. 9:3). If animals are designated for various sacrifices, the power of the act of designation is taken for granted; so too is the force of the law governing a given sacrifice. If therefore one designates an animal for a sacrifice, and that animal, in fact, cannot serve for the specified sacrificial purpose, the status of the animal has to be worked out (M. Pes. 9:7). Still more interesting is the case in which an animal is designated for a given sacrifice but then becomes confused with other animals. The status of the whole herd or flock then has to be adjudicated (M. Pes. 9:8, among many instances, and see the whole tractate of Qinnim). These are examples of the way in which cases of irreconcilable doubt are formed.

The Importance of Resolving Doubts

The Mishnah above all presents a protracted exercise in problems of practical logic and their solutions, applying conflicting principles. The Mishnah as a document is made up of studies in the potentialities of applied and practical reason. The Mishnah therefore accomplishes far more than merely providing well-organized information about topics important to the priests, transactions critical to the householders, and procedures and modes of expression of the scribes. As I have now shown through extensive allusions to all Divisions and topics of the Mishnah, the Mishnah has its own method of analysis; its generative problematic far transcends the topics of interest to its several distinct tributaries. It is in this method of sorting out confused things that the Mishnah becomes truly Mishnaic, distinct from modes of thought and perspective to be assigned to groups represented in the document.

To interpret the meaning of the facts just now described, we must once again recall that the priestly code makes the point that a well-ordered society on earth, with its center and point of reference at the Temple altar, corresponds to a well-ordered canopy of heaven. Creation comes to its climax at the perfect rest marked by completion and signifying perfection and sanctification. Indeed, the creation myth represents as the occasion for sanctification a perfected world at rest, with all things in their rightful place. Now the Mishnah takes up this conviction, which is located at the deepest structures of the metaphysic of the framers of the priestly code and, therefore, of their earliest continuators and imitators in the Mishnaic code. But the Mishnah frames the conviction that in order is salvation, not through a myth of creation and a description of a cult of precise and perfect order. True, the Mishnah imposes order upon the world through lines of structure emanating from the cult. The Scripture selected as authoritative leaves no alternative. Yet, as we have now seen, the Mishnah at its deepest layers, taking up the raw materials of concern of priests and framers and scribes, phrases that concern after the manner of philosophers. That is to say, the framers of the Mishnah speak of the physics of mixtures, conflicts of principles which must be sorted out, areas of doubt generated by confusion. The detritus of a world seeking order but suffering chaos now is reduced to the construction of intellect.

If, therefore, we wish to characterize the Mishnah when it is cogent and distinctive, and not merely the artifact of perspectives of distinct groups, we must point to this persistent and pervasive mode of thought. For the Mishnah takes up a vast corpus of facts and treats these facts, so to speak, "Mishnaically," that is, in a way distinctive to the Mishnah, predictable and typical of the Mishnah. That is what I mean when I refer to the style of the Mishnah; its manner of exegesis of a topic, its mode of thought about any subject, the sorts of perplexities which will precipitate the Mishnah's fertilizing flood of problem-making ingenuity. Confusion and conflict will trigger the Mishnah's power to control conflict by showing its limits, and, thus, the range of shared conviction too.

For by treating facts "Mishnaically," the Mishnah establishes boundaries around, and pathways through, confusion. It lays out roads to guide people by ranges of doubt. Consequently, the Mishnah's mode of control over the chaos of conflicting principles, the confusion of doubt, the improbabilities of a world out of alignment is to delimit and demarcate. By exploring the range of interstitial conflict through its ubiquitous disputes, the Mishnah keeps conflict under control. It so preserves that larger range of agreement, that pervasive and shared conviction, which is never expressed, which is always instantiated, and which, above all, is forever taken for granted. The Mishnah's deepest convictions about what lies beyond confusion and conflict are never spelled out; they lie in the preliminary, unstated exercise prior to the commencement of a sustained exercise of inquiry, a tractate. They are the things we know before we take up that exercise and study that tractate.

Now all of this vast complex of methods and styles, some of them intellectual, some of them literary and formal, may be captured in the Mishnah's treatment of its own, self-generated conflicts of principles, its search for gray areas of the law. It also may be clearly discerned in the Mishnah's sustained interest in those excluded middles it makes up for the purpose of showing the limits of the law, the confluence and conflict of laws. It further may be perceived in the Mishnah's recurrent exercise in the study of types of mixtures, the ways distinct components of an entity may be joined together, may be deemed separate from one another, may be shown to be fused, or may be shown to share some traits and not others. Finally, the Mishnah's power to sort out matters of confusion will be clearly visible in its repeated statement of the principles by which cases of doubt are to be resolved. A survey of these four modes of thought thus shows us one side of the distinctive and typical character of the Mishnah, when the Mishnah transcends the program of facts, forms, and favored perspectives of its tributaries. We now turn to the side of the substance. What causes and resolves confusion and chaos is the power of the Israelite's will. As is said in the context of measurements for minimum quantities to be subject to uncleanness, "All accords with the measure of the man" (M. Kel. 17:11).

The Catalyst: Sanctification and Man's Will

The Mishnah's principal message, which makes the Judaism of this document and of its social components distinctive and cogent, is that man* is at the center of creation, the head of all creatures upon earth, corresponding to God in heaven, in whose image man is made. The way in which the Mishnah makes this simple and fundamental statement is to impute power to man to inaugurate and initiate those corresponding processes, sanctification and uncleanness, which play so critical a role in the Mishnah's account of reality. The will of man, expressed through the deed of man, is the active power in the world. Will and deed constitute those actors of creation which work upon neutral realms, subject to either sanctification or uncleanness: the Temple and table, the field and family, the altar and hearth, woman, time, space, transactions in the material world and in the world above as well. An object, a substance, a transaction, even a phrase or a sentence is inert but may be made holy, when the interplay of the will and deed of man arouses or generates its potential to be sanctified. Each may be treated as ordinary or (where relevant) made unclean by the neglect of the will and inattentive act of man. Just as the entire system of uncleanness and holiness awaits the intervention of man, which imparts the capacity to become unclean upon what was formerly inert, or which removes the capacity to impart cleanness from what was formerly in its natural and puissant condition, so in the other ranges of reality, man is at the center on earth, just as is God in heaven. Man is counterpart and partner and creation, in that, like God he has power over the status and condition of creation, putting everything in its proper place, calling everything by its rightful name.

So, stated briefly, the question taken up by the Mishnah is, What can a man do? And the answer laid down by the Mishnah is, Man, through will and deed, is master of this world, the measure of all things. Since when the Mishnah thinks of man, it means the Israelite, who is the subject and actor of its system, the statement is clear. This man is Israel, who can do what he wills. In the aftermath of the two wars, the message of the Mishnah cannot have proved more pertinent—or poignant and tragic.

Now these statements of generalities take on meaning only when fully illustrated and exemplified in the details of the Mishnaic law. For, as we now know full well, while the Mishnah takes up a dense program of philosophical convictions, and while both in form and in substance the Mishnah assumes a position on a vast range of perennial issues of

---

* The patriarchal character of the Mishnaic system requires this usage and no other. It would be misrepresented if I were to speak of men and women, even though for certain purposes women are actors and participants.

the mind, still, the Mishnah also, and always, is little more than a mass of specific problems, a morass of concrete details, exercises of logic, and facts. So it is not possible to repeat what the Mishnah wishes to say without confronting the message in the Mishnah's own mode of formulation and expression. Through the medium of law the Mishnah says what it wants to say to its age and about its world. That is why, as has been the case up to now, we turn to the myriad of instances in which a single thing is said.

Reflection on the Nature of Intention

The principal message of the Mishnah is that the will of man affects the material reality of the world and governs the working of those forces, visible or not, which express and effect the sanctification of creation and of Israel alike. This message comes to the surface in countless ways. At the outset a simple example of the supernatural power of man's intention suffices to show the basic power of the Israelite's will to change concrete, tangible facts.

The power of the human will is nowhere more effective than in the cult, where, under certain circumstances, what a person is thinking is more important than what he does. The basic point is that if an animal is designated for a given purpose, but the priest prepares the animal with the thought in mind that the beast serves some other sacrificial purpose, then, in some instances, in particular involving a sin offering and a Passover on the fourteenth of Nisan, the sacrifice is ruined. In this matter of preparation of the animal, moreover, are involved the deeds of slaughtering the beast, collecting, conveying, and tossing the blood on the altar, that is, the principal priestly deeds of sacrifice. Again, if the priest has in mind, when doing these deeds, to offer up the parts to be offered up on the altar, or to eat the parts to be eaten by the priest, in some location other than the proper one (the altar, the courtyard, respectively), or at some time other than the requisite one (the next few hours), the rite is spoiled, the meat must be thrown out. Now that is the case, even if the priest did not do what he was thinking of doing. Here again we have a testimony to the fundamental importance imputed to what a person is thinking, even over what he actually does, in critical aspects of the holy life (see M. Zeb. 1:1–4:6; M. Men. 1:1–4:5; Neusner, *Holy Things* I, pp. 12–90, II, pp. 9–76).

The power of a person to impose the status of sanctity upon an object also is best illustrated in the case of the cult. If a person sets aside an animal for a given sacrifice, the animal becomes holy and is subject to the rules governing that sacrifice for which it is designated. This exercise of the will, therefore, has a material effect upon the status and disposition of the animal. That principle circulates throughout all the laws governing the sacrificial process and is illustrated in countless problems (see M. Pes. 9:7, 8; M. Zeb. 1:1ff., etc.). The critical role of human attentiveness in forming a context of cultic cleanness, moreover, is expressed in the notion that if the person who has to bring the pure water to be used with the ash of the red cow for the making of purification water diverts his attention from his task in any way whatsoever, then the water is no longer suitable. That means that if he performs a single action not pertinent to the task of bringing the water, the water is automatically invalid. If, further, he should sit or lie on any object, even if the object is clean, he is deemed unclean for the present purpose. So he must be ever on the move, must not sit down or lie down, from the moment he gets the water to the time at which he mixes it with the ash (M. Par. 5:1–11:6). Truly is it said that attentiveness is the precondition of cleanness (M. Sot. 9:15). The water used for the purification rite must be drawn deliberately, by human action, with a utensil made by a human being (M. Par. 5:1ff.). Any act of labor extraneous to the work of drawing the water and mixing the water with the cow ash is going to invalidate the entire procedure (M. Par. 7:1–4).

Another instance in which the altitude of a person affects the material reality of the law concerns the use of the immersion pool. All of the flesh must be in contact with the water. If there is some sort of dirt or other object adhering to one's flesh, then it is deemed to interpose only if a person is fastidious about that dirt. If it is not something about which one might be concerned, then it also is deemed to be null, as if it were not there to begin with (M. Pes. 3:2; M. Miq. 9:3).

The definitive transfer of ownership of property takes place when the original owner has either willingly given over that object or despaired ever of regaining it. If, therefore, someone saves an object from a flood, if the owner has given up hope of getting the object back, the object belongs to the finder (M. B.Q. 10:2). If the owner still has hope of regaining it, or if the finder has reason to believe that that is the case, then transfer of ownership does not take place (see M. B.M. 2:1–2, 5, 6). So attitude is everything. Despair determines the cessation of rights of ownership.

A piece of wood carved in a form is not deemed an idol until it actually has been worshiped. One belonging to a gentile is deemed prohibited forthwith, since it is assumed to be venerated. But one belonging to an Israelite is forbidden only after the Israelite will have worshiped the object. So the expression of the Israelite's will transforms the inert object into an idol (M. A.Z. 4:4–6).

Given the power imputed to the human will or intention, we should expect that some sustained attention will focus upon the nature of will. True, we cannot expect the philosophers of the Mishnah to phrase their thought in terms readily accessible to us. Nor is it possible to claim that they undertook a sustained program of inquiry into this, to them critical, matter of the nature of the will. Still, we do find something akin to abstract thought on the subject albeit, as always, in the predictable grossly material costume. The inquiry into the nature of the human will is expressed in the question of whether we deem intention to be divisible or indivisible. That is, if one wants something at one time but not at some other, is that an effective act of will? Again, if one wants something with regard to some part of a mixture but not with regard to some other part, the rule has to be defined (M. Makh. 1:1–6). The basic point for imparting susceptibility to uncleanness, that water must be deliberately, that is, intentionally, applied to foodstuffs before they are deemed susceptible, thus generates numerous problems involving the assessment of the human will (M. Makh. 2:1–11). For instance, if water is used for one purpose, its status as to a secondary purpose has to be worked out. If one wets down a house to keep the dust down and wheat was put into the house and got damp, the purposive use of the water for one thing renders the water capable of imparting susceptibility to the grain too (M. Makh. 3:4–5:8). The available positions will maintain, in general, these views: First, what one does defines what one's intention was to begin with. What actually happens defines what one originally thought of doing. The opposite view is that not only action, but intention independent thereof, is determinative. There is a balance to be found between what one ultimately does and what to begin with one wanted to do.

Insight into the character of thought about the nature of human intention derives from diverse, concrete rules. One recurrent issue is whether we take account of what one wishes to do, or only what one actually has done, to confirm one's stated intention. Another is whether we trust a person's deed if the deed is reversible, or whether we deem a person's intention not confirmed until a deed has been done which cannot again be revised. This notion is expressed in the usual, quite odd settings (see, for example, M. Kel. 20:6). The issue of whether intention unratified by actual deed is effective is worked out, for example, in terms of purification water. If someone forms the intention to drink such water, even without doing so, by mere intent, in the opinion of some, he has invalidated the water. Others hold the water is made unfit only when the man actually picks up the cup to drink the water. But this still is before a physical action has affected the water (M. Par. 9:4). intention to use an object renders it susceptible to uncleanness as soon as the object is ready for use. That is the case, even though the object has not yet actually been used. This will account for the difference between hides belonging to householders, deemed ready for use even before completely tanned, and those belonging to a tanner, which are not fully processed. The former are susceptible as soon as the householder decides to make use of them, even if he has done nothing to them (M. Kel. 26:8; cf. M. Kel. 26:7).

The notion that a statement of the will of a person bears material consequences in the status of a thing is limited by the parallel notion that a person's will has bearing only on what falls within that person's domain (M. Ar. 1:1–2). Similarly, it is held that the altar sanctifies what is appropriate to it, and does not sanctify what is not appropriate to it. This is without regard to what man wills. The altar does not work automatically to impart sanctity to whatever touches it. There is a necessary congruity between a human act of sanctification and what is sanctified (M. Zeb. 9:1ff.). A further limitation on the power of the will, even of the centrality of right intention in doing a deed, is the position that the one who brings a sin offering must know precisely why he must do so, that is, for what sin or category of sin (M. Ker. 4:2–3). From these rather theoretical remarks, we turn to concrete exemplifications, in the detail of the law, of what intention or will or attitude can and cannot do.

The Power of Intention

Once man wants something, a system of the law begins to function. Intention has the power, in particular, to initiate the processes of sanctification. So the moment at which something becomes sacred and so falls under a range of severe penalties for misappropriation or requires a range of strict modes of attentiveness and protection for the preservation of cleanness is defined by the human will. Stated simply: at the center of the Mishnaic system is the notion that man has the power to inaugurate the work of sanctification, and the Mishnaic system states and restates that power.

This assessment of the positive power of the human will begins with the matter of uncleanness, the antonym, we recall, of sanctification or holiness. Man alone has the power to inaugurate the system of uncleanness. One striking example of that fact is that water in its natural state, not subjected to human intervention and therefore will, not only effects purification but, in requisite volume, is simply not susceptible to uncleanness at all. This means that water is susceptible only when a human being has so acted as to make it susceptible. That fact is congruent with the thesis that things which are not wet down by human action are not susceptible to uncleanness. What is dry is insusceptible. What is wet is susceptible only if a human being has made it wet. So at the foundations of the movement from cleanness to uncleanness and back is the intervention of purposeful human deed. What is a source of uncleanness comes from nature, is natural and not caused by human action. But what is susceptible is so, first, because it is useful to a human being; and, second, because it has been wet down by a human being (M. Makh. 1:1–6:3). To be deemed food and therefore to become subject to uncleanness, produce must be regarded by human beings as food. There are things which may or may not be food, with the result that, if people do not regard them as edible, they are not susceptible at all (M. Uqs. 3:1–3, 9). This affects market towns in which only Israelites shop; there forbidden items are not deemed food, because no one will imagine eating them.

From the power of man to introduce an object or substance into the processes of uncleanness, we turn to the corresponding power of man to sanctify an object or a substance. This is a much more subtle matter, but it also is more striking. It is the act of designation by a human being which "activates" that holiness inherent in crops from which no tithes have yet been set aside and removed. Once the human being has designated what is holy within the larger crop, then that designated portion of the crop gathers within itself the formerly diffused holiness and becomes holy, set aside for the use and benefit of the priest to whom it is given. So it is the interplay between the will of the farmer, who owns the crop, and the sanctity inherent in the whole batch of the crop itself which is required for the processes of sanctification to work themselves out. That is why, for example, the question of who has the power to set aside heave offering from a crop will receive sustained attention (see M. Ter. 1:1ff.). The principal point about the obligation to tithe a crop is that the crop must be ripe. God claims the produce when it is ripe, and man must satisfy that claim before he has a right to dispose of the remainder of the crop (M. Ma. 1:3; Jaffee, p. 2). The crop may be tithed when it is ripe. But the point at which it must be tithed comes only at a later time. The obligation to tithe is imposed by the farmer's own acts. He becomes obligated to separate tithes at that point at which the crop has been harvested and processed for storage. That is when the owner's intention to store the produce for use in food is fully ratified in deed. Since the owner has laid claim to the produce as his own and now plans to use it for a meal, he may not proceed with his now fully revealed plan until he has tithed the produce. In establishing his claim to the produce, thus in exposing his intention, he has imposed upon the produce the sanctity which also and concomitantly arouses the divine claim to what belongs to God (M. Ma. 1:5; Jaffee, p. 3). So the point at which the crop must be tithed corresponds to the moment at which the farmer's intentions are fully in effect. Once more we see that is the human will which activates or precipitates the actualization of the sanctity which inheres in the crop. Once a householder has decided to make use of a batch of produce for a meal, the produce may not be used as a snack unless it is first tithed. The intention to make a meal of the produce is determinative. All subsequent acts of eating carry out that original intention. The produce therefore must be tithed before it is eaten (M. Ma. 4). To be sure, actions therefore guide our interpretation of a householder's intentions and so determine whether the obligation to tithe applies. But the main point is that the formulation of the intention affects the liability of the produce, independent of anything the householder actually does (Jaffee, p. 233).

In addition to the power to initiate the process of sanctification and the system of uncleanness and cleanness, man has the power, through the working of his will, to differentiate one thing from another. The fundamental category into which an entity, which may be this or that, is to be placed is decided by the human will for that entity. Man exercises the power of categorization, so ends confusion. The consequence will be that, what man decides, heaven ratifies. Once man determines that something falls in one category and not another, the interest of heaven is provoked. Then misuse of that thing invokes heavenly penalties. So man's will has the capacity so to work as to engage the ratifying power of heaven.

Let us take up first of all the most striking example, the deed itself. It would be difficult to doubt that what one does determines the effect of what one does. But that position is rejected. The very valence and result of a deed depend, to begin with, on one's prior intent. The intent which leads a person to do a deed governs the culpability of the deed. There is no intrinsic weight to the deed itself. For example, one is not supposed to put out a fire on the Sabbath. If one puts out a lamp because one is afraid of gentiles, thugs, or an evil spirit, one is not culpable. If one did so to save the oil, lamp, or wick, one is liable. These latter actions are done for their own sake; the others, for an extrinsic consideration. An act of labor done for a motive which is not culpable, itself is not culpable (M. Shab. 2:5). If a person intended in doing an act to violate the law of the Sabbath but did not actually succeed in doing so, he is not culpable (M. Shab. 10:4, 11:6). For example, if he planned to carry an object in the normal way, which would then be culpable, but carried it in an unusual way, which is not culpable, he is not liable. If he performed a forbidden act of labor for some purpose other than the commission of that act of labor itself, he is not culpable (M. Shab. 10:5).

From the power of will over deed, we turn to the capacity of the human will to determine the status of a substance or an object. One instance is simple to grasp. If an object is useful, it is susceptible to uncleanness. If it is useless, it is deemed broken and therefore clean. The criterion of usefulness is expressed fully in accord with human convenience. A three-legged table which has lost a leg is insusceptible, so too if it loses a second leg. It will tip over. But if it loses a third leg, it is deemed a tray and useful once more. But at that point, the susceptibility of the tray, in the view of some, is made to rest upon whether it is automatically useful, or whether a person has to give thought to use the former three-legged table as a tray. The prior issue is whether the maker of the three-legged table had in mind more than that potential use. If we decide that, to begin with, the craftsman imagined that the surface of the table also might serve as a tray, then when the legs are removed, the surface automatically takes up the new purpose, foreseen by the craftsman, and is susceptible. Clearly, much thought on the nature and working of human purpose and intention has gone into the formulation of these problems and their numerous parallels (M. Kel. 22:2; cf. M. Kel. 25:9). Further distinction is made between primary and secondary purpose (M. Kel. 22:7). If there is a rag which may or may not be useful, then, if it is kept in readiness for a particular purpose, it is susceptible to uncleanness, and if not, it is not susceptible. The difference is that in the former case, the rag serves some purpose useful to human need or intention, and that is signified by its being set aside for a given use (M. Kel. 28:5).

When utensils are broken, they are deemed no longer unclean, or (if they were not unclean to begin with) insusceptible to uncleanness. As I said, the criterion for breakage is uselessness. Once a utensil serves no purpose relevant to the needs of a human being, it is deemed useless and insusceptible. In consequence, there will be long lists of functions served by various utensils, with the notion that, so long as said utensils are sufficiently whole to serve these minimal functions, they are susceptible. All of these functions are relative to human need, measured by human estimation, and, immediately as well as ultimately, subject to the criterion of human purpose (see M. Kel. 14:1, 17:1–15).

Human will not only is definitive. It also provides the criterion for differentiation in cases of uncertainty or doubt. This is an overriding fact. That is why I insisted earlier that the principle range of questions addressed by the Mishnah—areas of doubt and uncertainty about status or taxonomy—provokes an encompassing response. This response, it now is clear, is the deep conviction of the Mishnaic law, present at the deepest structures of the law, that what man wills or thinks decides all issues of taxonomy. This claim on my part requires ample instantiation. It is the center of my thesis.

Where we have a gray area, the farmer's intention settles all issues. There are crops which may serve either for seed or for herbs. If the farmer sows the seed intending to produce a new crop, that is, to collect seed for future sowing, then even edible leaves which come up are not subject to the requirement of tithing; the plant is intended as other than food. If the farmer sows to harvest the crop for its leaves, even the seeds must be tithed. The seeds can be eaten and share the status of the leaves, for which the farmer planted the crop to begin with (M. Ma. 4:5–6). There are different removes of uncleanness, e.g., what is used for a utensil is susceptible to corpse uncleanness, while what is used for lying or sitting is susceptible to uncleanness imparted by the pressure or weight of certain unclean persons. Now a given object may serve for one or the other purpose, e.g., a head wrap, which may be used for an article of clothing or for a seat. The shift in human purpose for such an object will govern the remove of uncleanness to which it is susceptible (M. Kel. 24:1–15, 28:5).

It is in this context that we can take up the place of "the heart" or attitude and intention in matters of prayer and cultic liturgy. Without knowledge of the context just now reviewed, we might have deemed to be "natural" the importance imputed in the setting of divine service to right thinking. We now realize that that importance in the present case is in fact characteristic of the system which makes judgments such as these on the definitive and differentiating power of the human will or intention. If one was reading from the Torah those passages which contain the words of the *Shema'* at the very moment at which the obligation to say the *Shema'* pertained, one's reading of the passages may or may not be deemed to carry out that obligation. What makes the difference is whether or not the person intends his act of reading the words to constitute the recitation of the *Shema'* to which he is liable (M. Ber. 2:1). If a person merely believes that he is fit to serve as a priest at the altar, then his acts of service are valid. Once he discovers that he in fact is not fit to serve at the altar, any further acts of service will be invalid. So the person's own attitude toward himself governs the substantive value of what he has done at the altar (M. Ter. 8:1). One is supposed to pray facing the Temple. If one cannot do so, it suffices if one "directs one's heart" in that direction (M. Ber. 4:5–6).

At the same time, this power of sanctification through man's will itself will be regulated. Merely willing something is null, if, to begin with, one has not got the right to form an intention for a given thing. If one wills what is contrary to fact, one's intention is not effective. There must be a correspondence between what one wills and what one actually does, where a deed is required to ratify the stated intention. In these and other ways, when the householder wishes to separate heave offering, he must both form the appropriate intention to do so and orally announce that intention, designating the portion of the crop to be deemed holy (M. Ter. 3:8). Without both proper intention and proper deed, nothing has been done.

The power of intention is not only positive, in inaugurating the working of the Mishnah's system. It also is negative, and this is in four aspects.

First of all, if people regard an entity as null, useless, or without value, then the object plays no role in the law at all. So man's will has the power to remove an object or a substance from the system entirely, as we have already noted in a different context (see above, pp. 159f.). Something deemed useless or null by people is not going to be taken into account by the law. That applies, for example, to herbs or weeds which people do not cultivate. Whatever is not subject to the will and purpose of a human being is deemed to be of no effect (M. Sheb. 9:1). Mixtures of heave offering and unconsecrated produce take up a fair amount of attention (M. Ter. 4 and 5). When the heave offering is of a minute and negligible quantity, then it is deemed null and loses its power to impose prohibitions on the mixture of which it is a part (M. Ter. 4:7). If a transaction involving the redemption of produce in the status of second tithe is carried out unintentionally, it is null, and there has been no transfer of sanctity (M. M.S. 1:5–6). Vows made under constraint or in error are null. Merely uttering the formulary of a vow is not binding, without an appropriate intent's being expressed by that formulary (M. Ned. 3:3, 4; M. Naz. 5:1–7). If a person intends to say one thing but says another, what he has said is null. Words are of effect only when they express what the person intended to say (M. Ter. 3:8).

Second, the absence of human intervention is just as critical as its presence. When the law wishes to restore conditions to their natural state, it requires nature, without man's participation, for the work. That is why water to be used for an immersion pool cannot be gathered, that is, may not be subjected to human intention and will. It must gather on its own, flow naturally (M. Miq. 2:4–5:6). When he uses an immersion pool, those bodily adherences or excretions about which a person is fastidious are deemed to interpose. If a person does not take them into account, then they will not be taken into account in the system of cleanness (M. Miq. 9:1–7).

Conclusion

The characteristic mode of thought of the Mishnah is to try to sort things out, exploring the limits of conflict and the range of consensus. The one thing which the Mishnah's framers predictably want to know concerns what falls between two established categories or rules, the gray area of the law, the excluded middle among entities, whether persons, places, or things. This obsession with the liminal or marginal comes to its climax and fulfillment in the remarkably wide-ranging inquiry into the nature of mixtures, whether these are mixtures of substances in a concrete framework or of principles and rules in an abstract one. So the question is fully phrased by both the style of the Mishnaic discourse and its rhetoric. It then is fully answered. The question of how we know what something is, the way in which we assign to its proper frame and category what crosses the lines between categories, is settled by what the Israelite man wants, thinks, hopes, believes, and how he so acts as to indicate his attitude. With the question properly phrased in the style and mode of Mishnaic thought and discourse; the answer is not difficult to express. What makes the difference, what sets things into their proper category and resolves those gray areas of confusion and conflict formed when simple principles intersect and produce dispute, is man's will; Israel's despair or hope is the definitive and differentiating criterion.

Now the definition of what we mean when we speak of will, let alone attitude, intention, purpose, hope, and despair, should not be thought obvious or easy to locate. For it is not. In fact I have spoken of a number of distinct, if interrelated, matters: intellect and heart, a mixture of mind and feeling, a confusion of attitude and desire. Indeed, what is confusing in the Mishnah's understanding of the power of the human will is its capacity to deem as one entity mixtures of mind and heart, intellect and emotion, attitude and expectation. None of these is ever fully sorted out. Perhaps it is the Mishnah's founders' deepest conviction that they should not be sorted out. At any rate, I cannot try. So far as I can see, what the Mishnah wishes to say by a range of words, such as *kawwanah* (intention); *rasson* (will or desire); the very common word choice, *mahsshabah* (thought, attitude, or intention)— these are references to diverse sides of a very large but single thing: mind and heart. Perhaps in other times and other places our description might demand that we call this thing the soul. But for our purposes, the work is done when we show the single place and a single function of mind and will and demonstrate, as I have, that in the Mishnaic system man's feelings and powers to reflect bear power over the material world. This power, it turns out, is what sustains the entire structure and moves and motivates the working of the cogent system conceived by the framers of the Mishnah. The single word, intention, thus is made, only for convenience's sake, to cover multiple modes by which the human will comes to full expression and reaches its richest range of power.

The Mishnah's evidence presents a Judaism which at its foundations and through all of its parts deals with a single fundamental question: What can a man do? The evidence of the Mishnah points to a Judaism which answers that question simply: Man, like God, makes the world work. If man wills it, nothing is impossible. When man wills it, all things fall subject to that web of intangible status and incorporeal reality, with a right place for all things, each after its kind, all bearing their proper names, described by the simple word, sanctification. The world is inert and neutral. Man by his word and will initiates the processes which force things to find their rightful place on one side or the other of the frontier, the definitive category, holiness. That is the substance of the Judaism of the Mishnah.

So the Mishnah's style sets the question, and the substance of the Mishnah's laws answers it. The Mishnah's mode of thought and its manner of exegesis of its topics lay out the issues. Through its message the Mishnah disposes of those issues by introducing the critical and decisive role of the human disposition. This will of man is what differentiates. This intention of man has the power of taxonomy. The Mishnah's Judaism is a system built to celebrate that power of man to form intention, willfully to make the world with full deliberation, in entire awareness, through decision and articulated intent. So does the Mishnah assess the condition of Israel, defeated and helpless, yet in its Land; without power, yet hóly; lacking all focus, in no particular place, certainly without Jerusalem, yet set apart from the nations. This message of the Mishnah clashes with a reality itself cacophonous, full of dissonance and disorder. The evidence of the Mishnah points to a Judaism defiant of the human condition of Israel, triumphant over the circumstance of subjugation and humiliation, thus surpassing all reality. All of this is to be through the act of Israel's own mind and heart.

Abbreviations

Ah. Ahilot
Ar. Arakhin
A. Z. Abodah Zarah
B. Babylonian Talmud
B. B. Baba Batra
Bekh. Bekhorot
Ber. Berakhot
Bik. Bikkurim
B. M. Baba Mesia
B. Q. Baba Qamma
1 Chr. 1 Chronicles
2 Chr. 2 Chronicles
Dem. Demai
Deut. Deuteronomy
Ed. Eduyot
E. J. Encyclopaedia Judaica. Jerusalem, 1971.
Erub. Erubin
Ex. Exodus
Ezek. Ezekiel
Gen. Genesis
Git. Gittin
Hag. Hagigah
Hal. Hallah
Hor. Horayot
Hul. Hullin
Is. Isaiah
Jer. Jeremiah
Kel. Kelim
Ker. Keritot
Ket. Ketubot

Kil. Kilayim
Lev. Leviticus
M. Mishnah
Ma. Maaserot
Mak. Makkot
Makh. Makhshirin
Me. Meilah
Meg. Megillah
Men. Menahot
Mid. Middot
Miq. Miqvaot
M. Q. Moed Qatan
M. S. Maaser Sheni
Naz. Nazir
Ned. Nedarim
Neg. Negaim
Nid. Niddah
Num. Numbers
Oh. Ohalot
Or. Orlah
Par. Parah
Pe. Peah
Pes. Pesahim
Pr. Proverbs
Ps. Psalms
Qin. Qinnim
R. H. Rosh Hashanah
San. Sanhedrin
Shab. Shabbat
Shebu. Shebuot
Sheb. Shebiit
Sheq. Sheqalim
Sot. Sotah
Suk. Sukkah
T. Tosefta
Ta. Taanit
Tam. Tamid
Tem. Temurah
Ter. Terumot
Toh. Tohorot
T. Y. Tebul Yom
Uqs. Uqsin
Y. Yerushalmi. Palestinian Talmud
Yad. Yadayim

Yeb. Yebamot
Y. T. Yom Tob
Zab. Zabim
Zeb. Zebahim

Bibliography

Joseph Agassi. "Conventions of Knowledge in Talmudic Law." In Jackson, *Studies*. Pp. 16–34.

Hanokh Albeck. *Seder Mo'ed*. Jerusalem and Tel Aviv, 1954.

———. *Seder Nashim*. Jerusalem and Tel Aviv, 1954.

———. *Seder Neziqin*. Jerusalem and Tel Aviv, 1959.

———. *Seder Qodoshim*. Jerusalem and Tel Aviv, 1959.

———. *Seder Tohorot*. Jerusalem and Tel Aviv, 1958.

———. *Seder Zera'im*. Jerusalem and Tel Aviv, 1957.

Gedalyahu Alon. *Jews, Judaism, and the Classical World*. Jerusalem: Hebrew University, Magnes Press, 1977.

Aufstieg und Niedergang der römischen Welt: Geschichte und Kultur Roms im Spiegel der neueren Forschung. (*ANRW*) Vol. 1: ed. Hildegard Temporini. Vol 2: ed. Wolfgang Haase. Berlin and New York: De Gruyter, 1972–.

Ernst Bammel. "Die Blutgerichtsbarkeit in der römischen Provinz Judäa vor dem ersten jüdischen Aufstand." In Jackson, *Studies*. Pp. 35–49.

R. A. Bartels. "Law and Sin in 4 Esdras and St. Paul." *Lutheran Quarterly* 1 (1949): 319–29.

J. A. Bewer. Review of Moore, *Judaism*. *N.Y. Herald Tribune* (Books), 12 June 1927. P. 2.

J. Bloch. "Ezra Apocalypse: Was It Written in Hebrew, Greek or Aramaic?" *Jewish Quarterly Review* n.s. 48 (1958): 279–94.

———. "Some Christological Interpolations in the Ezra-Apocalypse." *Harvard Theological Review* 51 (1958): 87–94.

Francis W. Boelter. "Sepphoris, Seat of the Galilean Sanhedrin." *Explor* 3 (1977): 36–43.

P. M. Bogaert. *Apocalypse du Baruch: Introduction, traduction du Syriaque et commentaire*. Paris, 1969. Vols. 1 and 2.

———. "La Ruine de Jérusalem et les apocalypses juives aprés 70."

In *Apocalypses et théologie de l'espérance: Congrès de Toulouse (1975)*. Paris: Les Éditions du Cerf, 1977. Pp. 124–41.

———. "Le Nom de Baruch dans la littérature pseudépigraphique: L'Apocalypse syriaque et le livre deutérocanonique." In *Unnik: La Littérature juive*. Leiden, 1974. Pp. 56–72.

Baruch M. Bokser. "An Annotated Bibliographical Guide to the Study of the Palestinian Talmud." *ANRW*. Pp. 139–256.

———. "Samuel's Commentary on the Mishnah: Its Nature, Forms, and Content." In *AJS Newsletter,* 16 February 1976.

———. "Talmudic Form Criticism." *Journal of Jewish Studies,* 1980.

———. "Jacob N. Epstein's *Introduction to the Text of the Mishnah,*" "Jacob N. Epstein on the formation of the Mishnah," and "Y. I. Halevy." In Neusner, *Modern Study*. Pp. 13–36, 37–55, 135–54.

———. "Philo's Description of Jewish Practices." Center for Hermeneutical Studies in Hellenistic and Modern Culture. Protocol of the Thirtieth Colloquy. Ed. Wilhelm Wuellner. Berkeley, 1977.

———. "Reflections from Jewish Sources on the Religious Crisis of the Third Century" [= a "Response"]. In Peter Brown, *A Social Context to the Religious Crisis of the Third Century A.D.* Center for Hermeneutical Studies in Hellenistic and Modern Culture. Protocol of the Fourteenth Colloquy: Feb. 9, 1975. Ed. Wilhelm Wuellner. Berkeley, 1975. Pp. 19–24.

———. *Samuel's Commentary on the Mishnah: Its Nature, Forms, and Content. Pt. 1. Samuel in Berakhot*. Leiden: E. J. Brill. 1975.

———. "Two Traditions of Samuel: Evaluating Alternative Versions." In Jacob Neusner, *Christianity*. 4:46–55.

George Herbert Box. *The Ezra Apocalypse*. 1912.

D. Boyarin. "Penitential Liturgy in 4 Ezra." *Journal for the Study of Judaism* 3 (1972): 30–34.

E. Breech. "These Fragments I Have Shored Against My Ruins: The Form and Function of 4 Ezra." *Journal of Biblical Literature* 92 (1973): 267–74.

Otto J. Brendel. *Prolegomena to the Study of Roman Art*. New Haven and London: Yale University Press, 1979.

Peter Brown. "Understanding Islam." *New York Review of Books,* 22 February 1979.

F. C. Burkitt. "Baruch, Apocalypse of." In J. Hastings, ed., *Dictionary of the Apostolic Church*. 1915–18. 1:142–44.

S. J. Case. Review of Moore, *Judaism. Nation,* 24 August 1927.

Karen Chandler. "History of Religions in Gnostic Studies." Unpublished MS., 1979.

R. H. Charles and W. O. E. Oesterley. *The Apocalypse of Baruch*. London, 1929.

James H. Charlesworth. "Seminar Report: The SNTS Pseudepigrapha

Seminars at Tübingen and Paris on the Books of Enoch." *New Testament Studies* 25:315–23.

———. "Haplography and Philology: A Study of Ode of Solomon 16:8." *New Testament Studies* 25:221–27.

———. *The Pseudepigrapha and Modern Research.* Missoula: Scholars Press, 1980.

———. "Seminar Report. Reflections on the SNTS Pseudepigrapha Seminar at Duke on the Testaments of the Twelve Patriarchs." *New Testament Studies* 23:296–304.

———. Review of Alden Lloyd Thompson, *Responsibility for Evil in the Theodicy of IV Ezra. Journal of Biblical Literature* 98 (1979): 465–67.

Glenn F. Chesnut. *The First Christian Histories: Eusebius, Socrates, Sozomen, Theodoret, and Evagrius.* Paris: Éditions Beauchesne, 1977. Théologie Historique 46.

R. J. Coggins and M. A. Knibb. *The First and Second Books of Esdras.* Cambridge, 1979.

B. Cohen. Review of Moore, *Judaism. World Tomorrow* 10 (December 1927): 521.

Cesare Colafemmina. "Un nuovo ipogeo cristiano a Venosa." *Rivista de Teologia Ecumenico Patristica* 3 (1975): 159–68.

———. "Iscrizioni paleocristiane di Venosa." *Vetera Christianorum* 13 (1976): 149–65.

———. "Nuove scoperte nella catacomba ebraica di Venosa." *Vetera Christianorum* 15 (1978): 369–81.

———. ed. *Studi storici.* Molfetta, 1974.

———. "Un 'iscrizione venosina inedita dell' 822." *Rassegna Mensile d'Israel* 43 (1977): 261–63.

G. Dautzenberg. "Das Bild der Prophetie im 4 Esra und im Syr. Bar." *Urchristliche Prophetie: Ihre Erforschung, ihre Voraussetzungen im Judentum und ihre Struktur im ersten Korintherbrief.* BWANT Folge 6. Heft 4. Stuttgart, 1975. Pp. 90–98.

Albert-Marie Denis. *Introduction aux pseudépigraphes grecs d'Ancien Testament.* Leiden, 1970. Studia in Veteris Testamenti Pseudepigrapha. Vol. 1.

William Dever. In *Biblical Archaeologist* 43, no. 1 (1980).

Bruno W. Dombrowski. "*Hayyahad* and *To Koinón:* An Instance of Early Greek and Jewish Synthesis." *Harvard Theological Review* 59 (1966): 293–307.

A. M. Duff. *Freedmen in the Early Roman Empire.* 2d ed. Oxford, 1958.

Richard Duncan-Jones. *The Economy of the Roman Empire.* Cambridge, 1974.

Samuel K. Eddy. *The King Is Dead: Studies in the Near Eastern*

Resistance to Hellenism, 334–31 B.C. Lincoln: University of Nebraska Press, 1961.

Howard Essner. "Orlah: A Commentary." In Green, *Approaches* III.

V. Fàbrega. *Das Endgericht in der syrischen Baruchapokalypse.* Innsbruck, 1969.

Arthur Ferch. "The Two Eons and the Messiah in Pseudo-Philo, 4 Ezra, and 2 Baruch." *Andrews University Seminary Studies* 15 (1977): 135–52.

M. I. Finley. *The Ancient Economy.* Berkeley and Los Angeles: University of California Press, 1973.

Joel D. Gereboff. "The Pioneer: Zecharias Frankel," "Hirsch Mendel Pineles: The First Critical Exegete," "Joachim Oppenheim." In Neusner, *Modern Study.* Pp. 59–75, 90–104, 155–66, 180–96.

————. *Rabbi Tarfon: The Tradition, the Man, and Early Rabbinic Judaism.* Missoula: Scholars Press, 1979.

S. Gero. " 'My Son the Messiah': A Note on 4 Esra 28–29." *Zeitschrift für die Neutestamentliche Wissenschaft* 66 (1975): 264–67.

Robert Goldenberg. "The Broken Axis: Rabbinic Judaism and the Fall of Jerusalem." *Journal of the American Academy of Religion. Supplement.* 45 (1977): 869–82.

————. "Commandment and Consciousness in Talmudic Thought." *Harvard Theological Review* 68 (1975): 261–71.

————. "The Deposition of Rabban Gamaliel II." *Journal of Jewish Studies* 23 (1972): 167–90.

————. "The Historical Study of Jewish Law." *AJS Newsletter* 22 (1978): 13–14, 19.

————. *The Sabbath-Law of Rabbi Meir.* Missoula: Scholars Press, 1979.

————. "The Ethical Categories of Reinhold Niebuhr." *Conservative Judaism* 22 (1967): 67–74.

————. "The Jewish Sabbath in the Roman World." *ANRW.* II. 19.1.

————. "B. M. Lewin and the Saboraic Element," "Jacob B. Epstein," and "David Weiss Halivni, *Meqorot uMesorot: Ketuvot.*" In Neusner, *Formation.* Pp. 51–60, 75–86, 134–147.

David Goodblatt. "The Beruriah Traditions." *Journal of Jewish Studies* 26 (1975): 58–85.

————. "Bibliography on Rabbinic Judaism." In Jacob Neusner, ed., *Understanding Rabbinic Judaism: From Talmudic to Modern Times.* New York: KTAV, 1974. Pp. 383–402.

————. "Historiography in the Service of Text Criticism." *AJS Newsletter* 24 (1979): 17.

————. *Rabbinic Instruction in Sassanian Babylonia.* Leiden: E. J. Brill, 1974.

————. "The Origins of Roman Recognition of the Palestinian Patriarchate." *Studies in the History of the Jewish People and the Land of Israel*. Vol. 4. Haifa, 1978. Pp. 89–102.

——. *Reader on the History of the Jews in Parthian and Sassanian Mesopotamia*. Haifa: University of Haifa Student Union, 1976.

——. *Reader on Jewish Sects in Late Antiquity*. Haifa: University of Haifa Student Union, 1974.

——. "The Talmudic Sources on the Origins of Organized Jewish Education." *Studies in the History of the Jewish People and the Land of Israel*. Vol. 5. Haifa, 1980.

——. "The Babylonian Talmud." *ANRW*. Pp. 257–336.

——. "Y. I. Halevy," "Abraham Weiss: The Search for Literary Forms," and "David Weiss Halivni, *Meqorot uMesorot: Gittin*." In Neusner, *Formation*. Pp. 95–103, 164–74, 246–47.

——. "Local Traditions in the Babylonian Talmud." *Hebrew Union College Annual* 98 (1977): 60–90.

Leonard Gordon. "Shebiit: A Commentary." Unpublished Ms.

William S. Green. "Palestinian Holy Men: Charismatic Leadership and Rabbinic Tradition." *ANRW*. Pp. 619–47.

——, ed. *Approaches to Ancient Judaism*. Missoula: Scholars Press, 1978.

——, ed. *Approaches to Ancient Judaism*. Vol. 2. Missoula: Scholars Press, 1980.

——, ed. *Approaches to Ancient Judaism*. Vol. 3. Chicago: Scholars Press, 1981.

——, trans. (with W. J. Sullivan). Renée Bloch, "Methodological Note for the Study of Rabbinic Literature." In Green, *Approaches* I. Pp. 29–50.

——. "Context and Meaning in Rabbinic Biography." In Green, *Approaches* II.

——. *The Traditions of Joshua ben Hananiah*. Part 1: *The Early Traditions*. Leiden: E. J. Brill, 1981.

——. "The Talmudic Historians: N. Krochmal, H. Graetz, I. H. Weiss, and Z. Jawits," "J. S. Zuri," and "Abraham Goldberg." In Neusner, *Modern Study*. Pp. 107–21, 169–79, 225–41.

——. "What's in a Name—The Problematic of Rabbinic 'Biography.' " In Green, *Approaches* I.

——, ed. *Persons and Institutions in Early Rabbinic Judaism*. Missoula: Scholars Press, 1977.

Joshua M. Grintz. "Baruch, Apocalypse of." *EJ* 4:270–72.

Dennis Groh. "Galilee and the Eastern Roman Empire in Late Antiquity." *Explor* 3 (1977): 78–92.

Léon Gry. *Les Dires Prophétiques d'Esdras (IVe d'Esdras)*. Vols. 1 and 2, Paris, 1938.

———. "La 'Mort du Messie' en IV Esdras, VII, 29 [III, v. 4]." *Mémorial Lagrange*. Paris, 1940. Pp. 133–39.

Peter Haas. "Maaser Sheni: A Commentary." Unpublished Ms.

P. Hadfield. "Resurrection Body." *Church Quarterly Review* 158 (1957): 296–305.

J. Hadot. "Le Problème de l'Apocalypse syriaque de Baruch d'après un ouvrage récent." *Semitica* 20 (1970): 59–76.

———. "La Datation de l'Apocalypse syriaque de Baruch." *Semitica* 15 (1965): 79–95.

William W. Hallo. "New Moons and Sabbaths: A Case-Study in the Contrastive Approach." *Hebrew Union College Annual* 48 (1977): 1–18.

Wolfgang Harnisch. *Verhängnis und Verheissung der Geschichte: Untersuchungen zum Zeit und Geschichtsverständnis im 4. Buch Esra und in der Syr Baruchapokalypse*. Göttingen, 1969.

Daniel J. Harrington and Maurya P. Horgan. "Palestinian Adaptations of Biblical Narratives and Prophecies." Unpublished Ms.

Abraham Havivi, "Hallah Chapters 1 and 2: A Commentary." In Green, *Approaches* III.

A. P. Hayman. "The Problem of Pseudanonymity in the Ezra Apocalypse." *Journal for the Study of Judaism* 6 (1975): 47–56.

Joseph Heinemann. "Early *Halakhah* in the Palestinian Targumim." In Jackson, *Studies*. Pp. 114–22.

Joseph Heinemann. *Prayer in the Talmud: Forms and Patterns*. Trans. Richard S. Sarason. Berlin: de Gruyter, 1977.

Martin Hengel. *Acts and the History of Earliest Christianity*. Trans. John Bowden. London: SCM Press, 1979.

A. Hertzberg, ed. *Judaism*. New York, 1963.

Sidney Homer. Review of Moore, *Judaism. Boston Transcript*, 16 April 1927.

W. Lee Humphreys. *Crisis and Story: Introduction to the Old Testament*. Palo Alto: Mayfield, 1979.

Bernard S. Jackson. "The Fence-Breaker and the *actio de pastu pecoris* in Early Jewish Law. In Jackson, *Studies*. Pp. 123–36.

———. "History, Dogmatics, and Halakhah." Unpublished Ms., 1979.

———. "On the Problem of Roman Influence on the *Halakhah* and Normative Self-Definition in Judaism." Unpublished Ms., 1979.

———. *Structuralism and Legal Theory*. Liverpool: Liverpool Polytechnic Department of Law, 1979. Occasional Paper 20.

———. *Studies in Jewish Legal History in Honour of David Daube*. *Journal of Jewish Studies* 25 (February 1974).

J. A. Jackson, ed. *Social Stratification*. London, 1968.

Howard Jacobson. "Note on the Greek Apocalypse of Baruch." *Journal for the Study of Judaism* 7 (1976): 201–203.

Martin Jaffee. "Maaserot: A Commentary." Unpublished Ms.

Horace M. Kallen. "A Contradiction in Terms." [Review of Moore, *Judaism*] *Menorah Journal* 13 (1927): 479–86.

Armand Kaminka. "Beiträge zur Erklärung der Esra-Apokalypse und zur Rekonstruktion ihres hebräischen Urtextes." *Monatsschrift für Geschichte und Wissenschaft des Judentums* 76 (1932): 121–38, 206–12, 494–511, 604–607; 77 (1933): 339–55.

Shamai Kanter. "I. H. Weiss and J. S. Zuri," "Abraham Weiss: Source Criticism," and "David Weiss Halivni, *Meqorot uMesorot:* Qiddushin." In Neusner, *Formation.* Pp. 11–25, 87–94, 148–63.

Steven A. Kaufman. "The Structure of the Deuteronomic Law." *Maarav* 1 (1978–79): 105–58.

J. M. Kelly. *Roman Litigation.* Oxford, 1966.

A. F. J. Klijn. "Sources and the Redaction of the Syriac Apocalypse of Baruch." *Journal for the Study of Judaism* 1 (1970): 65–76.

A. C. B. Kolenkow. "Introduction to II Baruch 53:56–74: Structure and Substance." *Harvard Theological Review* 65 (1972): 597–98.

A. T. Kraabel. "The Diaspora Synagogue: Achaeological and Epigraphic Evidence since Sukenik." *ANRW.* II.19.1. Pp. 477–510.

———. "Social Systems of Six Diaspora Synagogues (with one plan)." Prepared for the SBL/AAR section, "Art and the Bible," under the theme "Ancient Synagogues: The Current State of Research." Unpublished Ms., 1979.

G. M. Lee. "Apocryphal Cats: Baruch 6." *Vetus Testamentum* 21 (1971): 111–12.

Baruch A. Levine. *In the Presence of the Lord.* Leiden: E. J. Brill, 1974.

J. S. Licht. "Ezra, 4 Ezra, Apocalypse of Ezra." *Encyclopedia Miqra'ith* (1971) 6:155–60.

———. *The Book of the Apocalypse of Ezra.* Jerusalem, 1968.

Jack N. Lightstone. "The Development of the Biblical Canon in Late Antique Judaism: Prolegomenon toward a Reassessment." *Studies in Religion,* 1979.

———. "Yosé the Galilean in Mishnah-Tosefta and the History of Early Rabbinic Judaism." *Journal of Jewish Studies,* 1979.

———. "Judaism of the Second Commonwealth: Toward the Reform of the Scholarly Tradition." In H. Joseph, J. Lightstone, M. Oppenheim, eds., *Truth and Compassion. Essays in Judaism and Religion for Rabbi Solomon Frank at 80,* Waterloo: Wilfred Laurier Press, 1983.

———. "Oral Torah in the Eyes of the Midrashists: Toward an Under-

standing of the Method and Message of the Halakic Midrashim."
Studies in Religion, 1980.

———. "Sadducees versus Pharisees: The Tannaitic Sources." In
Neusner, *Christianity*. 3:206–17.

———. "R. Sadoq." In W. S. Green, ed., *Persons and Institutions in
Early Rabbinic Judaism*. Missoula: Scholars Press, 1977. Pp. 49–
148.

———. *Yosé the Galilean: I. Traditions in Mishnah-Tosefta*. Leiden,
E. J. Brill, 1979.

Raphael Loewe. "Rabbi Joshua ben Hananiah: LL.D. or D. Litt.?" In
Jackson, *Studies*. Pp. 137–54.

Ulrich Luck. "Das Weltverständnis in der jüdischen Apokalyptik.
Dargestellt am Athiopischen Henoch und am 4 Esra." *Zeitschrift für
Theologie und Kirche* 73 (1976): 283–305.

Ramsay MacMullen. *Roman Social Relations, 50 B.C. to A.D. 284*. New
Haven, 1974.

Irving Mandelbaum. "Kilaim: A Commentary." Unpublished Ms.

T. H. Marshall. *Citizenship and Social Class and Other Essays*.
Cambridge, 1950.

W. D. MacHardy et al. "The Second Book of Esdras." *The New
English Bible with the Apocrypha*. New York, 1971. Pp. 19–53.

Wayne A. Meeks and Robert L. Wilken. *Jews and Christians in
Antioch in the First Four Centuries of the Common Era*. Missoula:
Scholars Press, 1978.

Y. Meshorer. "Sepphoris and Rome." In *Greek Numismatics and
Archaeology: Essays in Honor of Margaret Thompson*. Wetteren,
Belgium, 1979. Pp. 159–71 and plates.

Bruce M. Metzger. "Lost Section of II Esdras; i.e., IV Ezra." *Journal
of Biblical Literature* (1957): 153–56.

———. "The Fourth Book of Ezra and 2 Baruch." In "The Pseudepigrapha of the Old Testament," ed. J. H. Charlesworth. Unpublished
Ms.

Eric M. Meyers, A. T. Kraabel, and J. F. Strange. "Archaeology and
Rabbinic Tradition at Khirbet Shema: 1970 and 1971 Campaigns."
Biblical Archaeologist 35 (1972): 2–31.

———. "The Theological Implication of an Ancient Jewish Burial
Custom." *Jewish Quarterly Review* 72 (1971): 95–119.

———. "Galilean Regionalism as a Factor in Historical Reconstruction." *Bulletin of the American School of Oriental Research* 221
(1976): 93–101.

———, et al. "The Meiron Excavation Project: Archaeological Survey
in Galilee and Golan, 1976." *Bulletin of the American School of
Oriental Research* 230 (1978): 1–22.

Eric M. Meyers, C. Meyers, and J. F. Strange. *Report on the Excava-*

tions at Ancient Meiron, 1971–77. Vols. 3–4 of Meiron Excavation Project Series, 1980.

Eric M. Meyers et al. "Preliminary Report on the 1977 and 1978 Seasons at Gush Halav (el Jish)." *Bulletin of the American School of Oriental Research* 233 (1979): 33–58.

Eric M. Meyers. "The Cultural Setting of Galilee: The Case of Regionalism and Early Judaism." *ANRW* II. 19.1. Pp. 687–702.

Eric M. Meyers, A. T. Kraabel, and J. F. Strange. *Synagogue Excavations at Khirbet Shema'.* Duke University Press and Annual of the American School of Oriental Research No. 42. Durham, 1976.

Eric M. Meyers and J. F. Strange. "Survey in Galilee: 1976." *Explor* 3 (1977): 7–17.

Eric M. Meyers. "Galilean Synagogues and the Eastern Diaspora." Unpublished Ms., 1979.

Eric M. Meyers and J. F. Strange. *Archaeology, the Rabbis, and the New Testament.* Nashville: Abingdon, 1980.

Dean L. Moe. "The Cross and the Menorah." *Archaeology* 30 (1977): 148–57.

George Foot Moore. *Judaism in the First Centuries of the Christian Era: The Age of the Tannaim.* Vols. 1–3. Cambridge, Mass.: Harvard University Press, 1954. Orig. pub. 1927.

C. A. Moore. "Toward the Dating of the Book of Baruch." *Catholic Biblical Quarterly* 36 (1974): 312–20.

The Nag Hammadi Library in English. Translated by members of the Coptic Gnostic Library Project of the Institute for Antiquity and Christianity, James M. Robinson, director. San Francisco, 1977.

Jacob Neusner. *The Academic Study of Judaism.* Vols. 1–3. N.Y., 1975, 1977, 1980.

———. "The Formation of Rabbinic Judaism: Yavneh (Jamnia) from A.D. 70 to 100." *ANRW.* Pp. 3–42.

———. *Aphrahat and Judaism: The Christian-Jewish Argument in Fourth Century Iran.* Leiden, 1971.

———. *A History of the Mishnaic Law of Appointed Times.* Vols. 1–5. Leiden, 1981–82.

———, ed. *Christianity, Judaism, and Other Greco-Roman Cults: Studies for Morton Smith at Sixty.* Leiden: E. J. Brill, 1975.

———. "Comparing Judaisms: Essay-Review of *Paul and Palestinian Judaism* by E. P. Sanders." *History of Religions* 18 (1978): 177–91.

———. *A History of the Mishnaic Law of Damages.* Vols. 1–5. Leiden, 1982.

———. *Development of a Legend: Studies in the Traditions Concerning Yohanan ben Zakkai.* Leiden, 1970.

———. *Eliezer ben Hyracanus: The Tradition and the Man.* Vols. 1–3. Leiden, 1973.

———. *Form-Analysis and Exegesis: A Fresh Approach to the Interpretation of Mishnah* (Minneapolis, 1980).

———, ed. *The Formation of the Babylonian Talmud*. Leiden, 1970.

———. *A History of the Jews in Babylonia*. Vols. 1–5. Leiden, 1965–70.

———. *A History of the Mishnaic Law of Holy Things*. Vols. 1–6. Leiden, 1978–79.

———. *A Life of Yohanan ben Zakkai*. Leiden, 1970. Orig. pub. 1962.

———. "From Scripture to Mishnah: The Exegetical Origins of Maddaf." Fiftieth Anniversary Festschrift of the American Academy for Jewish Research. *Proceedings of the AAJR* (1979), pp. 99–111.

———. *Method and Meaning in Ancient Judaism: Essays on System and Order*. Missoula, 1979. Second Series: Chicago, 1980. Third Series: 1981.

———. *The Modern Study of the Mishnah*. Leiden, 1973.

———. "From Scripture to Mishnah: The Case of Niddah." *Journal of Jewish Studies* 29 (1978): 135–48.

———. *The Rabbinic Traditions about the Pharisees before 70*. Vols. 1–3. Leiden, 1971.

———. *The Idea of Purity in Ancient Judaism: The 1972–73 Haskell Lectures*. Leiden, 1973.

———. *A History of the Mishnaic Law of Purities*. Vols. 1–22. Leiden, 1974–77.

———. Review of *The Sages: Beliefs and Opinions*, by Ephraim E. Urbach. *Journal of Jewish Studies* 27 (1976): 23–35.

———. *After Historicism, beyond Structuralism: Story as History in Ancient Judaism*. Brunswick, Me.: Bowdoin College, 1980. The Spindel Memorial Lecture.

———. *The Tosefta: Translated from the Hebrew*. Vols. 2–6. New York, 1977–81.

———. *Way of Torah: An Introduction to Judaism*. 3d. ed. Belmont, 1979.

———. *A History of the Mishnaic Law of Women*. Vols. 1–5. Leiden, 1979–80.

G. W. E. Nickelsburg. "Narrative Traditions in the Paralipomena of Jeremiah and 2 Baruch." *Catholic Biblical Quarterly* 35 (1973): 60–68.

Arthur Darby Nock. *Essays on Religion and the Ancient World*. Selected and edited, with an introduction, bibliography of Nock's writings, and indexes, by Zeph Stewart. Vols. 1–2. Oxford: Clarendon Press, 1972.

Aharon Oppenheimer. "Jewish Settlement in Galilee in the Period of Yabneh and the Revolt of Bar Kokhba." *Qatedrah letoledot eres yisra'el veyishubah*. Jerusalem, 1977. 4:52–83.

S. Ossowski. *Class Structure in the Social Consciousness*. London, 1963.

Elaine Pagels. *The Gnostic Gospels*. New York: Random House, 1979.

Alan Peck. "Terumot: A Commentary." Unpublished Ms.

W. Pesch. "Die Abhängigkeit des II. salomonischen Psalms vom letzten Kapitel des Buches Baruch." *Zeitschrift für die alttestamentliche Wissenschaft* 67, nos. 3–4 (1955): 251–63.

M. Philonenko. "L'Âme à l'étroit." In *Hommages à A. Dupont-Sommer*. Paris, 1971. Pp. 421–28.

J. C. Picard. "Observations sur l'Apocalypse grecque de Baruch." *Semitica* 20 (2970): 77–103.

F. C. Porter. Review of Moore, *Judaism*. *Journal of Religion* 8 (January, 1928): 30–62.

Gary G. Porton. "The Artificial Dispute: Ishmael and Aqiba." In Neusner, *Christianity*. 4:18–29.

———. "According to Rabbi Y: A Palestinian Amoraic Form." In Green, *Approaches* I. Pp. 173–88.

———. *The Traditions of Rabbi Ishmael*. Pt. 1: *Non-Exegetical Materials*. Leiden: E. J. Brill, 1976.

———. *The Traditions of Rabbi Ishmael*. Pt. 2: *Exegetical Comments in Tannaitic Collections*. Leiden: E. J. Brill, 1977.

———. *The Traditions of Rabbi Ishmael*. Pt. 3: *Exegetical Comments in Amoraic Collections*. Leiden: E. J. Brill, 1979.

———. "Midrash: Palestinian Jews and the Hebrew Bible in the Greco-Roman Period." *ANRW*. Pp. 103–38.

———. "Jacob Brüll: The Mishnah as a Law-code," and "Hanokh Albeck on the Mishnah." In Neusner, *Modern Study*. Pp. 76–89, 209–24.

———. "Hanokh Albeck on the Talmudic Sugya." In Neusner, *Formation*. Pp. 127–133.

Charles Primus. *Aqiva's Contribution to Law of Zera'im*. Leiden: E. J. Brill, 1977.

———. "David Hoffman's 'The First Mishnah,' " "Abraham Weiss," and "Benjamin DeVries." In Neusner, *Modern Study*. Pp. 122–34, 197–208, 242–55.

Paul Radin. Review of Moore, *Judaism*. *New York Evening Post*, 23 April 1927. P. 5.

M. Rist. "Baruch, Apocalypse of." *International Dictionary of the Bible*. 1:361f.

Ellis Rivkin. *A Hidden Revolution: The Pharisees' Search for the Kingdom Within*. Nashville: Abingdon, 1978.

Ferdinand Rosenthal. *Vier apokryphische Bücher aus der Zeit und Schule R. Akiba's: Assumptio Mosis, Das vierte Buch Esra, Die Apokalypse Baruch, Das Buch Tobi*. Leipzig, 1885.

Margaret Wenig Rubenstein. "Bikkurim: A Commentary." In Green, *Approaches* III.

D. S. Russell. *The Method and Message of Jewish Apocalyptic.* London, 1964.

V. Ryssel. "Die syrische Baruchapokalypse." In E. Kautsch, *Die Apokryphen und Pseudepigraphen des Alten Testaments.* 1900. 2:406–446.

S. Sambursky, *Physics of the Stoics,* NY: Macmillan, 1959.

E. P. Sanders. *Paul and Palestinian Judaism.* London: SCM Press, 1977.

Richard Sarason. *A History of the Mishnaic Law of Agriculture: Section 3: A Study of Tractate Demai.* Part 1: *Commentary.* Leiden: E. J. Brill, 1979.

———. "On the Use of Method in the Modern Study of Jewish Liturgy." In Green, *Approaches* I. *Theory and Practice.* Pp. 97–172.

———. "Toward a New Agendum for the Study of Rabbinic Midrashic Literature." In Jacob J. Petuchowski and Ezra Fleischer, eds., *Joseph Heinemann Memorial Volume.* Cincinnati and Jerusalem: HUC Press and Magnes Press, 1981.

———. "Mishnah and Scripture: Preliminary Observations on the Law of Tithing in *Seder Zera'im,*" in Green, *Approaches* II.

———, ed. *The Modern Study of Midrash.* In progress.

Ernest W. Saunders. "Christian Synagogues and Jewish Christianity in Galilee." *Explor* 3 (1977): 70–77.

P. Schäfer. "Die Flucht Johanan b. Zakkais aus Jerusalem und die Gründung des'Lehrhauses' in Jabne." *ANRW.* Pp. 43–101.

Lawrence H. Schiffman. "Communal Meals at Qumran." *Revue de Qumran* 10 (1979): 45–56.

H. Schmid, "Baruch und ihm zugeschriebene Apokryphe und pseudepigraphische Literatur." *Judaica* 30 (1974): 54–70.

Carl E. Schorske. *Fin-de-Siècle Vienna: Politics and Culture.* New York: Knopf, 1980.

Samuel Schulman. Review of Moore, *Judaism. Jewish Quarterly Review* 18 (1927–1928): 339–55.

Emil Schürer. *A History of the Jewish People in the Time of Jesus Christ.* Second Division. III: *The Internal Condition of Palestine, and of the Jewish People, in the Time of Jesus Christ.* Trans. Sophia Tayler and Peter Christie. Edinburgh, 1886.

———. *The History of the Jewish People in the Age of Jesus Christ (175 B.C.–A.D. 135).* Vols. 1–2. Rev. and ed. by Geza Vermes and Fergus Millar. Edinburgh: T. & T. Clark, 1973.

J. Schwartz. "Sur la date de IV Esdras." In *Mélanges Andres Neher,* pp. 191–96.

Robin Scroggs. "The Sociological Interpretation of the New Testament: The Present State of Research." *New Testament Studies* 26 (1980): 164–79.

Johan Smertenko. Review of Moore, *Judaism. New York Times,* 19 June 1927. P. 5.

Jonathan Z. Smith. *Map Is Not Territory.* Leiden: E. J. Brill, 1977.

Morton Smith. *Jesus the Magician.* New York: Harper and Row, 1978.

———. *Palestinian Parties and Politics That Shaped the Old Testament.* New York: Columbia University Press, 1971.

Y. A. Solodukho. *Soviet Views of Talmudic Judaism. Five Papers by Yu. A. Solodukho.* Ed. Jacob Neusner. Leiden: E. J. Brill, 1973.

G. N. Stanton. "5 Ezra and Matthean Christianity in the Second Century." *Journal of Theological Studies* 28 (1977): 67–83.

Odil Steck. "Die Aufnahme von Genesis I in Jubiläen 2 und 4 Esra 6." *Journal for the Study of Judaism* 8 (1977): 154–82.

Wenzel Stoderl. *Zur Echtheitsfrage von Baruch I-III.* Vol. 8. Münster, 1922.

Michael E. Stone. "The Concept of the Messiah in IV Ezra." In *Religions in Antiquity: Essays in Memory of Erwin Ramsdell Goodenough,* ed. Jacob Neusner. Leiden, 1968. Pp. 295–314.

———. "Baruch, Book of." *Encyclopaedia Judaica* 4:272–73.

———. "Ezra, Apocalypse of." *Encyclopaedia Judaica* 6:1108–9.

———. *Features of the Eschatology of IV Ezra.* Ph.D. Dissertation, Harvard University, 1965.

———. "Some Remarks on the Textual Criticism of IV Ezra." *Harvard Theological Review* 60 (1967): 107–15.

Henry St. John Thackeray. *The Septuagint and Jewish Worship.* London, 1923. Pp. 80–111.

C. Thoma. "Jüdische Apokalyptik am Ende des ersten nachchristlichen Jahrhunderts: Religionsgeschichtliche Bemerkungen zur syrischen Baruchapokalypse und zum vierten Esrabuch." *Kairos* 11 (1969): 134–44.

A. L. Thompson. *Responsibility for Evil in the Theodicy of IV Ezra: A Study Illustrating the Significance of Form and Structure for the Meaning of the Book.* (SBLDS 29). Missoula: Scholars Press, 1977.

Joshua Trachtenberg. *Jewish Magic and Superstition.* Philadelphia, 1961. Jewish Publication Society of America.

E. Turdeanu. "L'Apocalypse de Baruch en slave." *Revue des etudes slaves* 48 (1969): 23–48.

E. E. Urbach. *The Sages: Their Concepts and Beliefs.* Trans. Israel Abrahams. Jerusalem: Magnes Press, 1969.

Geza Vermes. "Sectarian Matrimonial Halakhah in the Damascus Rule." In Jackson, *Studies.* Pp. 197–202.

———. *Scripture and Tradition in Judaism.* Leiden: E. J. Brill, 1961.

Theodor Wächter. *Reinheitsvorschriften im griechischen Kult.* Vol. 9. Giessen, 1910. *Religionsgeschichtliche Versuche und Vorarbeiten.*

Otto Wahl, ed. *Apocalypsis Esdrae; Apocalypsis Sedrach; Visio Beati Esdrae.* Leiden, 1977.

B. N. Wambacq. "L'Unité littéraire de Baruch I-III." *Bibliotheca Ephemeridum Theologicarum Lovaniensium* 12 (1959): 455–60.

――――. "Les Prières de Baruch I:15–II:19, et de Daniel IX: 5–19." *Biblica* 40 (1959): 463–475.

――――. "L'Unité du livre de Baruch." *Biblica* (1966). Pp. 574–76.

Kurt Weitzmann, ed. *The Age of Spirituality: Late Antique and Early Christian Art, Third to Seventh Century.* Catalogue of the exhibition at the Metropolitan Museum of Art, November 19, 1977 through February 12, 1978. Princeton: Princeton University Press, 1979.

R. McL. Wilson. *The Gnostic Problem: A Study of the Relations between Hellenistic Judaism and the Gnostic Heresy.* London, 1958.

Tzvee Zahavy. "Berakhot: A Commentary." Unpublished Ms.

――――. *The Traditions of Eleazar ben Azariah.* Missoula: Scholars Press, 1978.

F. Zimmerman. "Underlying Documents of IV Ezra." *Jewish Quarterly Review* 51 (1960) 107–34.